The Gurkha Rifles

J B R Nicholson • Illustrated by Michael Roffe

Series editor Martin Windrow

First published in 1974 by Osprey Publishing
Elms Court, Chapel Way, Botley, Oxford OX2 9LP,
United Kingdom
Email: **info@ospreypublishing.com**

ISBN 0 85045 196 5

A CIP catalogue record for this book is available from the
British Library.

Series editor: Martin Windrow

Printed in China through World Print Ltd.

04 05 06 07 08 10 9 8 7 6 5 4 3

**FOR A CATALOGUE OF ALL BOOKS PUBLISHED BY
OSPREY MILITARY AND AVIATION PLEASE CONTACT:**
The Marketing Manager, Osprey Direct UK
PO Box 140, Wellingborough, Northants
NN8 2FA, United Kingdom
Email: **info@ospreydirect.co.uk**

The Marketing Manager, Osprey Direct USA
c/o MBI Publishing, 729 Prospect Avenue
Osceola, WI 54020, USA
Email: **info@ospreydirectusa.com**

www.ospreypublishing.com

I am grateful to all those who have helped me compile this
brief and inadequate account of some outstanding soldiers.
It is not possible to mention them all – they range from the
unknown artist of our first illustration to the men who compiled
regimental histories, from those who took or carefully kept
old photographs to the compilers of dress regulations.
Amongst those living I would like to thank the National Army
Museum for their Patient assistance, notably Mr W. Y. Carman
for his book Indian Army Uniforms; Messrs R. J. Marrion and
D. S. V. Fosten who, in their special number of the magazine
Tradition, blazed a path; Mr A caton for invaluable assistance in
ferreting in general; Mr John Gaylor of the Military Historical
Society, who brought useful material to my notice, and of
course those who have permitted the use of illustrative material.
My greatest debt is to the officers and men of those Gurkha
regiments alongside whom I had the honour to serve, whose
efficiency and invariable cheerfulness I recollect with admiration.

Introduction

In present-day language the term 'Gurkha' is applied indiscriminately and inaccurately to the entire population of Nepal, although ethnographically the name should be applied only to the members of the old state of Goorkha which forms only a small part of the kingdom of Nepal. The Nepalese are divided into various clans and religions, as varied as any European country in their variety of accents and local dialects. There are the Aryan and Rajput clans which spread to Nepal during the fighting to suppress the Mongolians, bringing with them the Hinduism which supplanted Buddhism. Of the Mongolian tribes remaining in Nepal, the two major clans, the Magar and the Gurung, were both subdivided into many subclans or sects. In eastern Nepal two further tribes of Mongolian origin resided, the Limbos and the Rais. Those Nepalese of Aryan stock claiming Rajput descent are generally known as Khas Gurkhas, and include the Khas and Thakur tribes.

Nepal itself is an independent kingdom sandwiched between the north-eastern border of India and the mountains of Tibet. It occupies some 5,500 square miles along the Himalayas – a mountainous country with few roads. This terrain has affected the physical characteristics of the people, giving them the sturdy build and muscular legs developed by all hill peoples; and the Mongolian cast of features is unmistakable.

The Gurkhas have always got on extremely well with British troops and especially with Scottish Highlanders, with whom they seem to have a natural affinity. Their good humour is proverbial; and it is not without significance that it is said there are no locks in a Gurkha village.

(*A note on spelling*: many words which crop up repeatedly in this text are English transliterations from languages which are purely phonetic. Spellings have changed over the years, as English usage has changed – e.g. kukri, kukerie, khukri, Gurkha, Goorkha, etc. I have tried to be consistently inconsistent, by following the spelling of the period in question.)

Early History

In northern India the plains at the foot of the mountains between the Rivers Teesta and Sutlej had been occupied by a number of petty rulers who, during the course of the eighteenth century became nominal tributaries of the Mogul Emperor and received an equally nominal protection from aggression. From time immemorial it has been the custom for hill tribes to raid the peoples of the plains, and this area was no exception. Many of the hill tribes had managed to retain their independence both during and after the great expansion of the Mogul Empire, and the ruler of one of these tribes was the first to take note of and apply the lessons of the early British victories in Bengal. Prithi Narayan Sah was ruler of a small state situated to the north-west of Nepal, and, impressed by British success, he raised and disciplined a body of troops after the European fashion. The name of his little principality was Goorka.

When his troops were ready for action he proceeded to wage war upon his neighbours with remarkable success, and in 1762 had the satisfaction of trouncing the Nabob of Moorshedabad, Mir Cossim Ali, who had taken up the cudgels on behalf of some of the weaker local chiefs. An expedition mounted by the government of Bengal to assist the Rajah of Nepal was no more successful. Prithi Narayan Sah died in 1771, but his policies and methods were continued with equal success by his successors. The Gogra River was crossed

Group of Gurkhas in native dress, 1815; they are dressed almost entirely in white. The main interest lies in the variety of headgear, some of which appear a shade bizarre. The kukri is prominent among the weapons; note also the shield, which appeared as late as 1858 in the newly raised Hazara Battalion, later the 5th Gurkha Rifles. (India Office Library)

and the state of Kumaon seized, and attempts were even made to occupy Kashmir. When the kingdom of Oude finally came under British control, minor chieftains were left in undisturbed possession of their domains on payment of a fixed tribute. The method of the Gurkhas was slightly different. As each state was conquered the ruling family was exterminated and the Gurkhas usurped all rights and claims of the former rulers. It was inevitable that sooner or later they should come into contact with rulers who were in point of fact subjects of the British or under their protection. Thus endless complaints were made to the government, complaints treated with some degree of circumspection, since it was considered desirable to conciliate the Gurkhas. Their ruler was at this time a minor and the power of the state was in the hands of a powerful military clique of which the core was a family called Thappa. One member of the family, Bheem Sein, held the office of Prime Minister, while his brother, Umur Sing, was Commander-in-Chief of the army.

The Gurkhas were supremely self-confident. They themselves were unbeatable and their mountain fastnesses impregnable. The British presence caused them no qualms, and they saw no reason to abate their policy of expansion.

The Nepal War

It was during the second administration of Lord Cornwallis that the Gurkha tribes achieved well-nigh complete dominance over the territories bordering the frontiers of Nepal. Many of the local chiefs had, for a variety of reasons, become feudatories of the British, while the pacific attitude of the British virtually encouraged aggression. The Gurkhas raided at will and seized Bhootwal, an area on the borders of the kingdom of Oude. In 1813 the lion roared – the British demanded the immediate restoration of all occupied territories. The reply was a flat refusal. The new Governor-

General, Lord Moira, who had recently replaced Lord Minto, endeavoured to avoid conflict by further negotiation. The talks were abruptly terminated and the British envoys ordered to return, and a detachment of troops was dispatched from Goruchpoor to occupy the disputed territories. The force stayed for only a short period, during which native officials were appointed to administer the area, and then withdrew. As they withdrew the Gurkhas returned, and in Bhootwal surrounded three police stations, killed or wounded twenty-four of the defenders and murdered the local British officer. This was more than enough, and in November 1814 the Governor-General issued a declaration of war.

Some four divisions were assembled for the invasion numbering 22,000 men. A small detachment of 2,700 was provided for the defence of the frontier to the east of the Coosy River. The campaign opened with the Siege of Kalunga, a small hill fortress garrisoned by about 600 men.

Early Gurkha sepoy, c. 1816. The green uniform has black facings and lace, and the trousers are blue. The headgear seems to be a small round black cap with a small neat puggree, also black. Note the kukri, still worn in front as in civilian dress, and the *gurgabis* – native shoes. The musket seems to be a sawn-off Brown Bess. (National Army Museum)

An attempt at a frontal attack was repulsed with the serious loss of Major-General Rollo Gilespie, a notable soldier. After a prolonged artillery bombardment the garrison were compelled to evacuate, but not before inflicting heavy casualties on the besiegers.

The stout resistance of this force seems to have affected all but one of the remaining British commanders with a degree of caution approaching timidity. The exception was General Ochterlony. Ochterlony was cautious but thorough in his dealings with wavering chieftains, ruthless and thorough in dealing with the enemy. Several forts were reduced, and Umur Sing, Gurkha Commander-in-Chief, and brother of the Prime Minister, was forced to withdraw to a position at Maloun. This position was one flank of a line of fortified posts set upon a ridge which projected into the River Sutlej, and all the peaks intervening between the two flanks of this position, with the exception of two only, were occupied by strong stockades. The first position, the Ryla peak, Ochterlony seized without opposition, but the second, the Deothul, was taken only after a violent action on 15 April 1815. The following morning the Gurkhas threw in a ferocious counter-attack in a determined effort to recapture the peak, and despite the strengthening earthworks that the British had immediately dug, they succeeded in penetrating the defences in a number of places, although none proved decisive. The British artillery were subjected to a heavy volume of fire, so heavy that at one time there were no more than one bombardier and three British officers left to serve the guns. Fortunately for the British, reinforcements arrived from Ryla peak in time to turn the scales, and the Gurkhas were dispersed. They left behind some 500 dead. The British casualties were 213.

Meanwhile, other British columns were penetrating the state of Kumaon, still under Gurkha domination. A number of actions ended with the capture of the Setoli Heights, and the entire province was surrendered. The Gurkhas retired east of the Kalee River. The news of this victory most certainly contributed to the fall of Maloun, and the majority of the Gurkha officers and men surrendered despite all the efforts of Umur Sing. Left with no more than 250 followers, he realized

5

Excellent contemporary painting of the 1st Nasiri (Sabathu) Battalion in the 1820s. The uniform is rifle green with black collar, cuffs, and lace. The Gurkha officer appears to have silver-fringed wings; his trousers are grey-blue, his sash crimson, and his sword furniture and belt-plate brass. The shakos are black with black lace, cockades, etc. The belts, and the brush-and-picker cords, are black. The kukri is presumably worn on the right hip behind the pouch. (National Army Museum)

the hopelessness of his situation, and prudently surrendered. Territories were now restored to their rightful owners, and the whole region declared to be under British protection.

But the war was not yet over. The terms of peace proposed by Lord Hastings, now Governor-General, were refused, and General Ochterlony, now Sir David, took the field again with some 17,000 men in January 1816. He was in no way dismayed by the fact that the Gurkhas had fortified every recognized pass through the first range of hills. A deep ravine was found through which the British force wound its way to turn the enemy's position. The British marched up the valley of the Raptie and advanced upon Mukwanpoor, fighting a series of skirmishes *en route* which culminated in a general action in which the Gurkhas were defeated. At the news of this defeat the rejected treaty was accepted. The war was over, and from this travail the Gurkha regiments were born.

Early Years

Following the fall of Maloun in 1815 many of the Gurkha prisoners opted to enter the British service, and three battalions were formed – the First and Second Nasiri Battalions, and the Sirmoor Battalion. A fourth battalion was formed from the Gorakkpur hill regiments and was restyled the Kumaon Provincial Battalion. The Sirmoor Battalion had the distinction of being the first of these new units to see action in the British service, during the Mahratta War of 1817.

In 1824 the units received new and rather less interesting titles, the 1st and 2nd Nasiri Battalions becoming the 5th and 6th Local Battalions, and the Sirmoor and Kumaon Battalions becoming the 8th and 9th Local Battalions.

In 1825 Baldeo Sing, Rajah of Bhurtpore, died, leaving the throne to his young son, Balwant Sing, under the guidance of his uncle and guardian. Within a few weeks there was an uprising inspired by a nephew of the late Rajah, by name Doorjun Sal, which resulted in the murder of the uncle and his retinue and the imprisonment of the young Prince. The British Government, who had recognized the sovereignty of the young Prince, considered this as open defiance, and proceeded to take practical steps to restore him to his throne. Sir David Ochterlony immediately commenced preparations to march on Bhurtpore, but was restrained by Lord Amherst, the Governor-

General, who was alarmed at the already heavy expenditure caused by the Burmese War, and the memory of the galling defeat sustained at the last attempt upon the fortress of Bhurtpore. Doorjun Sal viewed this hesitation with some satisfaction, interpreting it as a sign of fear. He adopted a yet more truculent and intransigent posture, and, all attempts to negotiate having failed, a force of 21,000 men and 100 guns under the command of the Waterloo veteran, Lord Combermere, was dispatched to reduce the redoutable fortress. With the force were 100 men each of the Nasiri and the Sirmoor or 8th Local Battalion. The town was besieged, the walls mined and breached, and the garrison dispersed at bayonet point. This last operation was ably assisted by the 8th. The British force suffered some 600 casualties, while the enemy losses were estimated at 14,000. Doorjun Sal was cast into prison, and the young Rajah duly reinstated.

In the following year the 5th and 6th Local Battalions were re-formed as a single unit with the new title of 4th Local Battalion. By way of simplifying the historian's task the reshuffling permitted the 8th Local Battalion to become the 6th (Sirmoor) Local Battalion and the 9th to become the 7th (Kumaon) Local Battalion.

For the next twenty years there were few happenings of note, but in 1845 the Sikhs of the Punjab, who had long constituted a threat, finally boiled over into British territory. Ranjit Singh, the 'Lion of the Punjab', had established and ruled over a strong Sikh kingdom, maintaining it by sheer force of character. When he died the kingdom wallowed in a wave of intrigue and assassination. His successor, Kurruck Singh, was murdered, and scarcely were the funeral rites over when his son, No Nehal Singh, was deliberately crushed under a pile of bricks. As death followed upon death the entire Punjab sank into chaos, the divers factions having only one idea in common – hatred of the British. However, unified by this common hatred and with fears of British expansion by no means reduced by the widely reported views of Sir Charles Napier on the possibilities of war in the Punjab, a large Sikh army prepared for the passage of the Sutlej River, the border with British territory. These preparations were not unnoticed by the British command, and a force of 32,000 men with sixty-eight guns was assembled at Ferozepoor, Ludhiana, and Umbala. The Sikh Army crossed the river on 11 December 1845. The British held two positions, one at Ferozepoor, the other at Ferozshah, and at both earthworks were thrown up and every preparation for action set afoot. The Sikh passage of the Sutlej was greeted by an official declaration of war, and a column of troops dispatched from Bussean to Ferozepoor. This column reached Mudki, where reports were received that a Sikh encampment was close by. The column set off and after three miles' march came under artillery fire which was smartly returned. The Sikhs were then engaged with musketry and finally by the bayonet. The Sikhs withdrew, leaving some seventeen guns in British hands. But casualties were very heavy – 864 out of a total force of 1,200, and since no pursuit was possible, the Sikhs withdrew in reasonable comfort.

Three days later the Sikh encampment at Ferozshah was attacked, a force of 18,000 men and sixty-five guns attacking a Sikh force estimated at 35,000 and eighty-eight guns. After an initial artillery bombardment an infantry attack was launched, which had to be prematurely halted by nightfall. The Sikhs continued their bombardment, but the batteries were charged and the guns spiked. On the following day the attack was resumed with such success that seventy-six guns were captured and the enemy was forced to retire. Again heavy casualties made pursuit impossible, and the enemy were able to retire unmolested. British casualties are given as 2,400. Such heavy casualties in two engagements prevented a close pursuit to Lahore, and the

The belt-plate of the Sirmur Battalion, later 2nd Gurkha Rifles; of brass, this was worn on the right shoulder-belt.

enemy made full use of the lull while the British awaited reinforcements. A bridge of boats was thrown across the Sutlej and a fortified bridgehead established at Sobraon. Another force established itself in position at Aliwal near Ludhiana. A British force, which included men of the Sirmoor and Nasiri Battalions, marched off under the redoubtable Sir Harry Smith to the relief of Ludhiana; which accomplished, they set out for Aliwal. Following a brief bombardment, a charge was made by the 16th Lancers supported by the infantry. Some hard fighting followed in which the Sirmoors lost their colours temporarily. The Sikhs were finally driven back across the river and Sir Harry marched back to Ferozepoor and thence to Sobraon. (Curiously, I have read a report of the existence of a medal for Aliwal issued to a 5th Goorkha, a pretty problem to be unravelled.)

At Sobraon the Sikhs were entrenched in a truly formidable position – massive earthworks, a force estimated at 54,000 men, and seventy guns. The British force amounted to no more than 16,000 and ninety-nine guns. Battle was joined, and the assaulting forces beaten back again and again, but eventually the lines were cleared and a final cavalry charge threw the Sikhs back across the

The black regimental colour of the (later) 1st Gurkha Rifles. This dates from before 1850 when the regiment became the 66th or Goorkha Regiment, Bengal Native Infantry. (National Army Museum)

river. The British losses amounted to 2,383. Both Goorkha battalions were engaged in this fierce action, accompanying the force to Lahore, where finally the peace terms were agreed.

In 1848 the Second Sikh War, set off by the murder of two British officers, saw the British badly mauled at Chilianwala, but the final defeat of the Sikhs at Gujerat led to the annexation of the Punjab. Whilst the Goorkhas did not take part in the Second Sikh War, the annexation of the Punjab led eventually to the formation of the Punjab Frontier Force of which one regiment, the Hazara Goorkha Battalion, was to become the 5th Gurkha Rifles.

A typical piece of Treasury *chalarchi* was demonstrated with the annexation of the Punjab – the extra allowance formerly given to troops serving there was discontinued on the grounds that the country was no longer foreign duty. Needless to say, this miserable action caused great discontent, and there were rumours that the twenty-five regiments earmarked for service there were close to mutiny. Mutiny was avoided for a time, but some time later the 66th Bengal Native Infantry broke out and attempted to seize the fortress of Govidghur in which treasure to the tune of £100,000 was supposedly held. The mutiny was put down by the 1st Native Cavalry and the mutinous regiment packed off to Ambala where it was dis-

British officer, c. 1850 – this shows the typical Rifles dress of a British officer in the years before the Great Mutiny. It is first described in 1829 – see text – and the main changes since were in the head-dress and the cut of the trousers. Note the tassels of the crimson sash fastened at the left breast. The black ball tuft is not worn here.

missed from the service of the Honourable East India Company, and the 4th Local Battalion, now known as the 4th (or Nasiri) Rifle Battalion, who had escorted the mutineers from Ambala, was taken into the Line as the 66th or Goorkha Regiment, Bengal Native Infantry. This announcement is said to have caused scenes of great festivity and gratification since their pay as irregulars of four rupees eight annas per month was increased to the regular scale, the princely sum of seven rupees per month, plus the increased prestige of being Regulars.

After this mutiny, which took place in 1849, the new 66th settled down to normal peacetime soldiering. But this incident had been a warning. The hurricane was to come.

The Great Mutiny

The new Enfield rifle displeased nobody, but the greased cartridge was a different matter. Rumour had it that the cartridges were greased with a mixture of animals fats abhorrent to both Hindu and Muslim. By using it the Hindu would lose caste, and have to endure and pay for costly purification rites, while the Muslim would be seriously defiled. A perfect spark, whether true or not, to ignite the explosive situation which had been accumulating for years past, but this is not the place to try to unravel the twisted threads of this débâcle, when the great Bengal Army with its fine traditions dissolved in chaos.

First blood was drawn at Barrackpore on 29 March 1857 when Sepoy Mangal Pandy, whose name became the synonym for a mutinous sepoy as Tommy Atkins was to become that of a British soldier, wounded an officer and a sergeant who attempted to arrest him while he was exhorting other men to mutiny. The other sepoys refused to help. Pandy was sentenced and hanged, but the growing signs of unrest were unmistakable and the 19th Native Infantry were actually disbanded. But incendiary incidents and riots multiplied apace. On 3 May the 7th Native Infantry refused point-blank to use the new cartridges, and were disarmed. On 10 May the Meerut garrison broke into open revolt and were joined by the rabble

from the native bazaar in burning, looting, and pillaging. By the following evening Delhi was in the hands of the mutineers and the aged puppet Mogul Emperor became the symbol to whom the mutineers gave their allegiance. Too late now for the British to regret the shortsighted policy of not replacing the British troops dispatched to the Crimea.

The Gurkha regiments appeared unaffected, although some doubts were entertained. District Commissioner Greathead is quoted as having stated: 'We feel quite safe about the Gurkhas; their grog-drinking propensities are a great bond with the British soldier!' But despite this curious testimonial strong doubts were indeed entertained. A report that the Nasiri Battalion at Jutogh were in open mutiny started a panic at Simla, and even when the reports were proved unfounded the Gurkha guards were removed from the Treasury

This havildar of the Sirmoor Battalion wears a double-breasted coatee with black collar, cuffs, and buttons. Equipment appears to be white, and crossed belts are still worn. The regimental history states that on transfer to the Regular line in 1849 the corps was rearmed with a two-groove Brunswick rifle in place of the old smoothbore. For some reason the left shoulder-wing is omitted here. The sketch was published in 1857. (*Illustrated London News*)

and the entire battalion marched down to the plains, an action which infuriated the men. They demanded that as a gesture of confidence they should be put on guard at the bank, and some caustic remarks were made anent the safety precautions that the British residents were taking. But trouble did in fact break out at Kussowlie, where a party of Gurkhas robbed the Treasury and ran riot. A party of the 75th Foot were awaiting orders to proceed against them under a Captain Blackall when Mr Taylor, the Assistant Commissioner, succeeded in preventing precipitate action on the grounds that the safety of the community at Simla depended entirely upon preventing an escalation of the incident. Blackall contented himself with adopting purely defensive measures and ignoring the provocation. When the news reached General Anson, the Commander-in-Chief, the failure of the policy of disbanding disaffected regiments was painfully obvious. He selected an officer well versed in the habits and customs of the Gurkhas, and dispatched him to reason with them and to recall them to their allegiance. This officer, a Captain Briggs, was Superintendent of Roads. He was given plenary powers to secure his object at no matter what price. The price was a complete pardon, and this accorded, the result was complete success. There were no more signs of disaffection.

The hundredth anniversary of the famous Battle of Plassey was on 23 June 1857, an anniversary which, according to the strange rumours circulating throughout India was to mark the end of British rule. On that very anniversary the Gurkhas were in action on the famous Hindoo Rao ridge. The mutineers attacked from the Subzee Mundee suburb in an engagement lasting the better part of eleven hours. It was here, on the ridge before Delhi, that the lasting friendship between the 2nd Goorkhas and the 60th (the King's Royal Rifle Corps) was formed, and which led to the uniform of the 2nd Goorkhas being as similar as possible to that of the British regiment.

The regimental history of the 2nd gives many curious and interesting anecdotes, including one by General Lyte of the Royal Artillery who served at Delhi. The General relates that he was in conversation with Ensigns Wheatley and Foster near to where the colours of the Sirmoor Battalion stood against the wall with a sentry in front of them, when a round shot came through the veranda and cut the sentry in two. The next moment, before they had recovered from their astonishment and horror, the corporal of the guard stepped out and quietly posted another Gurkha sentry over the body of the dead one, which was then removed. Incidentally, a short time afterwards another round shot came through the wall, killing Wheatley and cutting the staff of the Sirmoor regimental colour in two.

On the final capture of Delhi, the Sirmoor Battalion, the only regiment of the entire force which was under fire and unrelieved for three months and eight days, was given the honour, together with the 60th, of garrisoning the Red Fort. As a further honour, a third colour was authorized and permission granted for three to be

Rifleman (left) of the Bengal Army, 1857, in typical Rifle costume of the period; note, however, the epaulettes worn instead of wings. The right-hand figure is a typical scarlet-coated sepoy of the Bengal infantry, with his brass *lota* or water- and cooking-pot on top of his pack. White linen covers are worn on the Kilmarnock caps. (*Illustrated London News*)

carried, contrary to the normal rule that Rifles carry no colours.

The Kumaon Battalion also served with distinction at Delhi, notably at the storming of the Kashmir Gate under Sir Colin Campbell, when John Nicholson received his mortal wound.

The Relief of Lucknow was notable for the presence in the force of no less than six battalions of Gurkhas; they distinguished themselves in that action, as well as serving in numerous minor engagements.

Post-Mutiny Expansion

From the Mutiny onwards the Gurkhas steadily expanded. The first new unit – the Extra Goorkha Regiment – was raised by Lieutenant MacIntyre in 1857, to become the 19th Bengal Native Infantry in 1861 when India was taken over by the Crown, at which time irregular units were taken into the line in replacement of the now vanished regiments which had mutinied or been disbanded.

In 1858 the Sirmoor Battalion received official recognition of its services at Delhi – the third colour, to be inscribed 'Delhi' in English, Persian, and Hindi, with special dispensation to carry colours in spite of the new designation of 'Sirmoor Rifle Regiment'.

The Gurkha units were now removed from the normal numbering of infantry of the line, and were placed in a separate category (1861) adding yet further confusion in following the regiments' careers; e.g. the 1st, who rejoiced in no less than ten changes of title between 1858 and 1936. (The various changes of designation are given in the Appendix at the end of this section.)

We have noted the extra colour of the Sirmoor Rifle Regiment. When the regiment was taken on the regular strength as a Rifle regiment it became subject to the rule that Rifles should not carry colours. The Queen, however, sent as an especial mark of favour, the silver truncheon, a unique trophy carried by the extra native officer formerly authorized for the third honorary colour, and accorded the same honours as the Queen's colour in line regiments. The old colours were kept in

the officers' mess until 1876 when they were made over to Sir Charles Reid, in whose possession they remained until presented to the Royal United Services Institute in 1893. It is interesting to note that these ancient colours (there were two sets) were carried by special permission by the Coronation contingent in 1902, His Majesty King Edward VII being Honorary Colonel of the regiment. The *Daily Telegraph* reported this unusual event as follows:

Then was seen for the first time that the Goorkhas were carrying once more their battered and bloodstained colours, which for almost forty years have reposed in the care of the Royal United Service Institute, but were now brought forth again by permission of the King. Faded and dim were these battle standards, but round them cling traditions that thrill the hearts of the heroic Goorkhas, of whom none of the present generation ever beheld the flags, which waved above their predecessors at Aliwal and Sobraon. There were two set of colours carried, the officers in charge being Captains H. D. Watson, A. B. Lindsay, D. M. Watt, and Subadar-Major Hastbir Gharte, Bahadur. The first set was carried by the 2nd Goorkhas from 1844 to 1850, and through the campaign on the Sutlej, 1845–46. Both were perforated with bullets and stained with blood. They were present when the Regiment saved the cantonment and city of Loodhiana, and in the subsequent defence of that city. They were carried at the battles of Bhuddiwal, Aliwal and Sobraon. At the latter battle the Regiment lost 145 killed and wounded – a quarter of its strength. In this action the colours were almost shot to pieces, and the shaft of the King's colour was cut in half by a cannon-ball; it was spliced on the field and still supports the colour. On the same day the Goorkha officer carrying the black Regimental colour was killed and the colour temporarily captured, and was recovered by the Goorkhas who cut their way into the midst of the enemy with great gallantry. The staff, which was not recovered, was immediately replaced by a bamboo cut on the field, and that bamboo is the one on which the remains of the colour are now attached. The second set, replacing the above worn-out ones, were carried by the Regiment from 1850 to 1863, and all through the Mutiny Campaign of 1857–59, when the Regiment lost more heavily than any other corps engaged.

These colours were carried throughout the

siege of Delhi, where the Regiment sustained and defeated twenty-six separate attacks on their post on the right of the Ridge, and in which they lost eight British officers killed and wounded out of nine engaged, and 327 out of 490 in the Goorkha ranks. Both colours are shot through and are bloodstained. The staff of the black Regimental flag was cut clean through by a 32-pounder shot, which killed and wounded one officer and nine men.

The Umbeyla Campaign

For the Pathan hill tribes warfare and feuding is a way of life involving raids, the burning of villages, and the elimination of enemies. Raids were normally short sharp actions, but in 1863 a sect known as the 'Sitana Fanatics' had grown so large, and their depredations so extensive that the government was forced into full-scale operations against them. During the Mutiny they had harboured many of the mutineers, and over a long period indulged themselves in guerrilla warfare against the British. The Yusafzai Field Force was organized and dispatched against them under the command of Sir Neville Chamberlain. The objective was to reach and destroy the main headquarters at a village called Malka to the north of the Mahaban mountain.

In order to reach the proposed base of operations for the expedition it was necessary to negotiate a range of mountains which had only one practicable pass. The pass was controlled by Bunerwal tribesmen, hostile to the Sitana Fanatics and from whom, in consequence, no opposition to the march through their territory was anticipated. One detail was overlooked – the little formality of informing the Bunerwalis. This proved a serious mistake, and the Sitana Fanatics had little difficulty in persuading them that the British advance was aimed equally at the permanent occupation of Bunerwal territory.

On 20 October 1863 Chamberlain entered the pass with his force which included the 4th Goorkhas. The first skirmish occurred two days later, and within a few days the whole of the Swat Valley was in arms. The British position was dangerous, stuck in a pass, unable to proceed and with lines of communication threatened. Their position was on a small plateau protected by pickets stationed on two flanking heights, of which one, known as the Crag, was a key position. The Crag was the scene of constant and bitter fighting, and on 13 November it was taken by the enemy and recovered only after two unsuccessful counterattacks. On the 20th the Crag was again lost, to be recovered by Chamberlain himself at the head of the 71st Highland Light Infantry and the 4th Goorkhas. The Crag was recovered with a loss of twenty-seven dead and 110 wounded, Chamberlain himself receiving the ninth wound of his career.

In December, reinforcements arrived and an advance was made through the pass. The tribes fell back and made a stand on a range of hills in front of the village of Umbeyla in the Chalma Valley, and were there defeated, and the village fired. This was enough, and the Bunerwalis sued for peace. The terms were agreeable – no less than to carry out the object of the British expedition and disperse the Sitana Fanatics and destroy Malka. This they accomplished in the presence of a small party of British officers sent as 'umpires' to this curious arrangement.

In 1866 the 2nd were again in action at Bhootan, as were the 4th, but in the meantime a most important decision had been made. Representations had been made to the Commander-in-Chief that the Gurkha soldiers were in effect aliens from their own country, and after a lifetime of service, seldom returned to the land of their birth. Hence it was most desirable that the Gurkhas should be allotted some permanent home in the land of their adoption where their families and a depot could be established during their absences on service. This was finally approved and in 1864 the 2nd were allotted permanently the lines occupied at Dehra Dun, while the 1st settled at Dhumsalla, the 3rd at Almorah, and the 4th at Bakloh. The 5th, part of the Frontier Force, finally settled at Abbottabad.

In 1871 the Black Mountain and Looshai operations engaged the 2nd and 4th in further tribal warfare.

In 1875 the first Gurkha force to serve overseas, the 1st, embarked for the Malay States where the British Resident had been murdered. Their

Subadar-Major carrying the Queen's Truncheon, *c.* 1863. This may be Singbir Thapa, senior Native officer of the 2nd Goorkha Regiment, one of the first Sirmoor Battalion enlistees in 1815. In 1814 he had been one of the garrison of Kalunga fort, which so gallantly resisted the British assaults until the last 80 survivors of the 700-man garrison cut their way out and escaped. In this picture the uniform is the rifle-green tunic and trousers and the Kilmarnock with red and black diced band. It is not possible to distinguish red piping down the front, but the General Order of 1858 authorizing uniforms the same as the 60th King's Royal Rifle Corps suggests this feature. The collar should thus be scarlet with black-laced edge, and the cuffs should have a three-point flap piped scarlet, and black lace edgings all round. Buttons appear bright metal here, but may have been blackened horn or metal which sometimes appear light in old photographs. Note the rank badges, crossed kukris edges downward, on the collar. The black shoulder-belt has bronze fittings, and the sword-belt probably had bronze mounts instead of the silver of other regiments. The medal ribbons are not clear, but the neck ribbon seems to be that of the Indian Order of Merit. No sword-knot is visible, but it should have been black. (Courtesy, R. G. Harris)

example was followed in 1878 by the 2nd who were posted to Malta in the Mediterranean during the Russo-Turkish War. They returned home just in time to participate in the Third Afghan War.

The 3rd Afghan War

Throughout the nineteenth century the British had an almost pathological fear of Russian expansion. Over the years the Russian frontier had steadily advanced towards India's northern borders. The Crimean War had cost Russia a great deal in terms of money and lost prestige, while suspected Russian influence in the Mutiny caused the British to eye with distrust every move or rumour in the north. Both sides took an active interest in the countries on their boundaries, Persia and Afghanistan in particular. When in 1878 a Russian envoy was received with every courtesy while the British envoy, Sir Neville Chamberlain, was rebuffed at the frontier, and

British and Native officers of the 44th (Sylhet) Regiment of Bengal Native (Light) Infantry, *c.* 1870. This group shows four British officers and five Native officers, with a general officer (or possibly a colonel on the staff) and a staff officer. The general (or colonel) wears the staff's dark blue patrol jacket with black braid and cord, and wide scarlet stripes on the overalls; the sword has a gold knot, and the slings two lines of gold embroidery. The blue cap has gold buttons, a gold lace band, and a gold-embroidered peak. The staff officer sitting on his right has a cap with gold-embroidered peak and black band, and a badge which is unfortunately not clear. His scarlet-welted trousers add to the mystery. The regimental officers, Nos. 3 and 4 from left, are distinguished by shoulder-belts. No. 3 wears the patrol jacket edged with black braid and with hip pockets, No. 4 the dress tunic. Belt fittings are silver. Nos. 1, 2, 5, 8, 9, and 10 wear rifle-green dress uniform with black facings including the false waistcoat to the Zouave jacket; note three-point, three-buttoned cuff flaps. Puttees are black, swords steel with steel scabbards; note that all waist-belts are worn under the tunic. Native officers' rank insignia, crossed kukris for subadars and single kukris for jemadars, are embroidered in silver on the right breast, as the Zouave jacket is collarless. The India General Service Medal is worn with the bar for Bhootan, December 1864–February 1866. Note that at this time only one company of the regiment was composed of Gurkhas; the bearded Native officers in the background are Hindustani Mussulmen (*cf.* Plate C3). (Courtesy, R. G. Harris)

repeated requests for an audience were ignored, British troops moved in to Afghanistan. The forces were divided into three columns – the Peshawur Valley Field Force under Lieutenant-General Sir Samuel Browne, V.C.; the Kurrum Valley Field Force under Major-General Sir Frederick Roberts, V.C.; and the Kandahar Field Force under Lieutenant-General Donald Stewart. The Peshawur Force crossed the border at Jamrud on 21 November, capturing Ali Masjid fort the following day. The 4th Goorkhas were with this column. The Kurram Force approached Peiwar Kotal to find the enemy had fortified the position in some depth and were manning it in force. Roberts attempted a most difficult manoeuvre – a night flanking march, leaving a small force working on gun positions to give the impression that a full-scale frontal attack was to be made. His main force attacked at daybreak on 2 December, supported by those left in position, and after some heavy fighting in which Captain John Cook of the 5th gained his V.C., the Afghans fled. British casualties were very light, ninety-eight, of whom ten only were killed. Roberts annexed the Kurram Valley, and Shere Ali hastened to Tashkent to enlist Russian aid. He got none, and his son, Yakoob Khan, negotiated a peace by which he accepted a British Resident at Kabul, the British were to occupy the Khyber Pass, the Kurram and Pisheen Valleys, and the Amir was to receive an annual subsidy of £60,000 and the promise of assistance in the event of aggression by another power.

The Resident, Sir Louis Cavagnari, reached Kabul on 24 July 1879 with an escort of Guides. On 3 September Sir Louis, his escort and all the other British residents of Kabul were murdered. (The escort received posthumous Orders of Merit to a man.)

Roberts was dispatched to Kabul, which he reached on 8 October, having defeated an Afghan force on the way at Charasia on the 6th, the 5th Goorkhas being present, and in company with the 92nd mounting the main assault on the right flank.

Remembering, perhaps, the débâcle of the First Afghan War, Roberts commenced to fortify a large area to the north of the city called Sherpur, a most prudent action, for in December he found himself under siege, supported by the 2nd, 4th, and 5th Goorkhas. The siege was soon lifted, and all was quiet awaiting a political decision. Before this was reached the storm broke. Ayub Khan seized power in Kandahar with the avowed intention of ousting the British, and, gathering a strong force of tribesmen, marched on the city. A British brigade under General Burrows engaged him with unfortunate results at Maiwand, and after losing a third of their strength were forced back to Kandahar which was immediately besieged by the elated tribesmen.

Roberts wasted no time, but set off and in twenty-one days covered the 313 miles to Kandahar. This was no agreeable jaunt, but 313 miles with the Afghans lurking to cut off stragglers and sniping into the column, through mountainous country with temperatures veering between 110° and freezing, and at last some thousand men being carried along racked with fever. On 1 September Roberts attacked, a flanking movement capturing the entire Afghan artillery, while the 2nd Goorkhas and the Gordon Highlanders contributed a magnificent head-on bayonet charge which nothing could withstand.

Burma 2nd Assam

In the years following, new formations of Goorkhas were raised. In 1886 the 42nd (Assam) Regiment of Bengal Light Infantry was redesignated as the 42nd Regiment Goorkha Light Infantry. This regiment had a long and honourable history from its foundation as the Cuttack Legion in 1817 at Orissa. When it was moved to north Bengal in 1823 its title was changed to Rangpur Light

Group from the 44th (Sylhet) Regiment, later the 8th Gurkha Rifles, c. 1875. A wide variety of costumes is shown here, ranging from the regimental mufti or civvies, to full dress. Nos. 1, 6, 7, and 13 from the left wear mufti – white shirt and trousers, white sash with the kukri tucked under it, blade edge uppermost, black civilian caps, and footwear which is not clear. Service dress or khaki drill, with black puttees and black leather equipment, is worn by Nos. 2, 17, and 19. It appears to have breast-pockets but no shoulder-straps or button, **except in the case of the Native officer, No. 20. Full-dress rifle-green faced black is worn by the remainder, except for No. 10, a British officer in a patrol jacket. For Native officers the black false waistcoat was edged at the front, but not at the top and bottom, with black braid. The three-point cuff flaps are also laced round with black braid – see Nos. 3 and 13. British and Native officers wear no cap badges, but other ranks wear a white metal '44'. The Enfield rifle was issued to the regiment in 1865. (Courtesy, R. G. Harris)**

15

Infantry Battalion, and in 1828 to the 8th (or Assam) Local Light Infantry Battalion; and having taken an active part in the First Burma War it was engaged in constant guerrilla warfare as a part of the permanent garrison of Assam. In 1886 two further regiments, the 42nd and 43rd of the Bengal establishment, were redesignated as Goorkha Light Infantry. The 43rd, raised as the Assam Sebundy Corps in 1835, had been transferred to the Bengal establishment in 1861 as the 47th Bengal Native Infantry, and almost immediately changed to 43rd. The 44th, raised as the 16th or Sylhet Local Battalion in 1824, became in 1861 the 48th Regiment Bengal Native Infantry, in the same year altered to 44th. Both regiments served in the Bhutan campaign of 1864–5.

The 43rd had an interesting adventure in 1891 when a detachment of the regiment was stationed on the North-eastern Frontier at Manipur, between Burma and Assam. During the previous autumn the Rajah had been overthrown and the British decided to intervene. Thus, in March 1891, some 400 Gurkhas marched with Assam's Chief Commissioner, J. W. Quintan, to reinforce a detachment of the 43rd who were employed as escort to the Political Officer, Mr F. Grimmond. The objective was the capture of the usurper, the commander of the Manipuri Army. In effect it was the Gurkhas who came under heavy attack. An attempt was made to parley, and the officer commanding the Gurkhas, the Commissioner, and the Political Officer proceeded to the palace at Imphal. They were seized and instantly killed. The Gurkhas, with whom was the unfortunate Political Officer's wife, succeeded in withdrawing, and retired towards Assam, falling in with another Gurkha detachment *en route* for Manipur. In the spring a strong British force marched on Imphal. It met with little opposition, and the rebel leader was captured, tried and hanged.

Chitral

Next to require attention was the State of Chitral. This small state was bordered to the south by Jandol, a small state whose ruler was somewhat less than friendly to the British. When the ruler of Chitral died in 1882 and the intrigues and assassinations which normally accompany such an event in that part of the world were in progress, Umra Khan of Jandol moved his army into Chitral. The British ordered him out, and dispatched a small force to make their point. The officer in charge of this force, Sir George Robertson, deposed the new ruler and replaced him by his younger brother. This failed to evoke any perceptible signs of satisfaction, and the force found themselves besieged in Chitral. News of this predicament had fortunately got through, and a relief force which included the second battalions of the 2nd, 3rd, and 5th Gurkhas, was mounted. On arrival it was found that a small column had already relieved the garrison, having fought their way through from Gilgit. A fort and garrison were established at Malakand, and this very fort was garrisoned by the 4th Gurkhas in the mid-1930s.

The Tirah Campaign

The year 1897 saw the North-west Frontier in a serious and widespread state of unrest, and in June and July there were fanatical outbreaks among the Waziris which culminated in a serious attack upon the local Political Officer and his escort in the Tochi Valley, while Malakand was attacked by the Mohmand and Swati tribes. In August the Afridis and the Orakzaies between Peshawur and Kohat became restless, and by the end of the month control of the vital Khyber Pass had been lost. The government was forced to act.

The forces assembled to deal with this serious situation included the Tirah Expeditionary Force, with the 2nd battalion 1st Gurkhas in the 1st Brigade of the 1st Division, and the 2nd battalion of the 4th in No. 6 Brigade, while the 1st battalion of the 3rd was with the 2nd Division. The Kurram Column included the 1st battalion of the 5th, while the 9th were with the Peshawur Column and the 2nd battalion of the 2nd were with the line of communication troops. Altogether an impressive turnout. Probably the most celebrated engagement of this expedition was the attack on the heights of Dargai in which the 3rd Gurkhas and the King's Own Scottish Borderers cleared a

The 2nd Goorkhas disembarking in Malta, 1878. An *Illustrated London News* engraving, interesting for the number of errors! The 'tourie' on the Kilmarnock has shrunk alarmingly: the jacket has acquired red piping, and a pointed cuff in place of the three-point flap: Native officers' rank-badges have been mistaken for regimental collar-badges and awarded to all ranks: and one havildar – sergeant – has reversed chevrons. Trouser-welts and button-spacing are equally fictitious. Red shoulder-straps have been recorded, but they had disappeared by the 1884 Regulations. (*Illustrated London News*)

strongly held ridge which the enemy were then allowed to reoccupy. The second attack met with yet stiffer opposition from an estimated 12,000 tribesmen, but the ridge was once more taken, and the Gordon Highlanders added one more honour to their proud history. The first man into the enemy position was in fact Subahdar Kirparam Thapa of the 2nd Goorkhas. The 2nd and the Gordons had established a most friendly relationship during the Afghan War, a friendship rendered yet firmer by the fact that, the 2nd being detailed to hold the ridge, their dead and wounded were carried back by the Highlanders. Briefly, the force advanced into the Maidan Valley, the very centre of the Tirah; the fertile lands were devastated and everything destroyed, for the force had to be withdrawn before the onset of the first snows. Before leaving the Maidan Valley, a sad little incident took place – in the words of the historian of the 2nd: 'Poor Wylie (Lieutenant, 2nd Goorkhas) and Lewarne, 15th Sikhs, who were brought in by the stretcher bearers of the Gordons, were buried at Maidan in the same grave, the last remaining piper of the Gordons playing a lament and Sir William Lockhart, with all available officers, being present. The signs of the grave were afterwards obliterated to avoid any possible desecration by the enemy, but bearings were taken for future identification.'

The withdrawal was not without incident. On 24 November the 2nd reached camp late in eighteen degrees of frost to find that the Gordons had already pitched their tents for them and were taking over their night duties.

The troops settled down for a winter of minor incidents, but with the taking of the Khyber, the force was dispersed. As the train containing the 2nd stopped at Rawalpindi, they were greeted by the Gordons who had assembled there to bid them farewell. On arrival home at Dehra Dun a pair of handsome kukries were ordered from Nepal and dispatched to the Gordons, one each for the officers' mess and the sergeants' mess. This handsome gesture was greatly appreciated, and the Gordons, not to be outdone in courtesy, returned the compliment by presenting the 2nd with a fine silver shield and statuette to serve as a musketry trophy.

The last years of the century saw much minor action in the Chin Hills, Chitral, and Waziristan and during the Boxer Rebellion in China, but the shape of the Indian Army was being changed.

Hitherto the armies of India had been separate armies, each pertaining to one of the three great presidencies, Bengal, Madras, and Bombay, together with some additional formations such as the Punjab Frontier Force – a small army of all arms. This was now considered archaic, inefficient, and wasteful, for while some units knew no peace, others mouldered away for generations without ever seeing more activity than a field day. In 1901, therefore, all regiments were placed on a single list and the old Presidency commands were replaced by a more practical tactical organization.

In 1903 there were further changes in numbering from which the Gurkha regiments, all now styled 'Rifles', appeared as a coherent organization outside the normal numbering of line infantry. There were now ten regiments:

> 1st Gurkha Rifles (the Malaun Regiment)
> 2nd (the Prince of Wales's Own) Gurkha Rifles (the Simoor Rifles)
> 3rd Gurkha Rifles
> 4th Gurkha Rifles
> 5th Gurkha Rifles (Frontier Force)
> 6th, 7th, 8th, 9th, and 10th Gurkha Rifles

The 6th was the former 42nd Bengal Native Infantry which had been designated Gurkha Rifles in 1901 and renumbered in 1903. Similarly the 7th and 8th had been the 43rd and 44th who had undergone the same process.

The 9th had first appeared as the Fatehgarh and Manupuri Levies, raised in 1817 and 1819, and had been taken on the strength of the Bengal Army in 1823, forming the nucleus for the 1st Battalion of the 32nd Bengal Native Infantry. In 1824 they had become the 63rd Regiment. They had performed nobly at Sobraon, capturing a standard. But at the time of the great Mutiny, the regiment was stood down despite a petition declaring their unshakable loyalty to the Raj. The regiment was reconstituted in 1861, and then renumbered as the 9th Regiment of Bengal Native Infantry, and first saw service in the Bhutan campaign of 1864. They played a minor part in the Third Afghan War, acquitting themselves with credit, and in 1888–9 took part in the Chin Lushai Expedition. Hitherto the regiment had been a mixed-class regiment of which one company only were Gurkhas. But in 1893 it was decided to have some single-class regiments and the 9th was composed of one class only – Khas Gurkhas. Newly formed, they took part in the Tirah campaign, and in 1901 were redesignated the 9th Gurkha Rifles.

The 10th had begun their career as the Kubo Valley Police Battalion, part of a force raised to guard the borders of Upper Burma in 1887. The unit was formed from volunteers from the Indian Army, including a considerable proportion of Gurkhas. In 1890 it was redesignated the 1st Regiment of Burma Infantry but changed in the following year to 10th Regiment (1st Burma Battalion) of Madras Infantry, under which title it also took part in the Chin Lushai Expedition. In 1901 the regiment became the 10th Gurkha Rifles.

Tibet 1903

At the turn of the century there were persistent rumours of increasing Russian influence in Tibet. So dangerous a situation could not be allowed to persist, and a mission of four diplomats with a small military escort set out for Khamba Jone just inside Tibet, and there settled down to await the arrival of Tibetan and Chinese delegates. They waited in vain and the mission was fruitless.

In the autumn the Tibetans arrested two alleged spies in the province of Sikkim, which, being Indian territory, was at the least illegal. The authorities took advantage of this situation to dispatch a small force into Tibet, albeit no further than Gyantse, some 100 miles short of the capital, Lhasa. By December the troops, including the 8th Gurkhas, were advancing through the Jelap La Pass under fearful conditions. The oil on the rifle-bolts froze, many of the pack-mules died, and despite the issue of special warm clothing, a number of the men were seriously affected by frostbite. The crossing of the border had been unopposed and no Tibetan forces were encountered until 31 March 1904 when a force of some 2,000 was found to have blocked and fortified the road at a village called Guru. The British commander, Colonel Younghusband, ordered his troops forward; the Tibetan commander replied by ordering them back. The British and Indian troops advanced slowly to within touching distance of the Tibetans. Younghusband ordered his men to disarm the enemy. When this had been partially accomplished the Tibetan commander ordered his troops to fire and a general engagement ensued. The British had two machine-guns, and in a short space of time the Tibetans had suffered some 900 casualties, while the British had six men wounded only.

The advance continued to Gyantze, where the force settled down to await delegates. Again none appeared, but a considerable Tibetan force did, and attacked with great vigour. During the subsequent action Lieutenant Grant of the 8th earned a V.C. Wounded while scaling a precipitous rock-face, down which he fell, he returned to the assault and so encouraged his men that the position was taken. The Tibetans were beaten off, and Younghusband was given grudging permission to advance on Lhasa. The force marched on and reached Lhasa on 2 August, and settled down to await the results of negotiations. In September terms were agreed, and considerable trading concessions made to the British. No evidence of the much-discussed Russian influence was to be found, and it appears that the rumours were the result of an innocent friendship between the Dalai Lhama and a Russian national.

In 1911 the 8th returned to the land of their (regimental) birth, Assam, there to operate against the Abor tribesmen. This was the year of the great Delhi Durbar of H.I.M. King George V, and only three years from the great conflagration that was to alter the face of the world.

The World Wars

So vast is the scope of the First World War that no more than the briefest mention can be made of the great events which were to occupy the years 1914 to 1918.

The 1st served in France, enduring the mud of Flanders trenches, excelling in no-man's-land patrols, and spreading the legend of the kukri abroad. In contrast the 3rd, who fought also in France, provided Lawrence of Arabia with mounted infantry, riding after the Turks on camels. The 2nd sent one battalion to France,

Interesting group of officers of the 4th Gurkha Regiment in hot-weather kit, 1878. The light khaki uniform, probably drill, is cut like a Norfolk jacket with pleats on either side of the breast; that on the left conceals a pocket which was apparently large enough for a revolver. Some have five visible buttons, some are concealed. Note the variety of gaiters, from short leather British infantry-style to suspiciously civilian-looking canvas, worn even with spurs by mounted officers. The black Sam Browne belt is worn in a number of ways; the sword, with leather-covered and steel-mounted scabbard, hangs in a frog, **apparently without a knot. White shirt collars are visible above the jacket collar, on which there is a suspicion of some piping. Revolver lanyards are worn. The officer standing on the right wears an entirely different patrol jacket of quite modern pattern; the tight lanyard makes it difficult to be certain but the collar may be of another colour. This garment is clearly of heavier material. The head-dress is the pillbox, stiff to the crown but with a soft top on which is a braided figure and a netted button; one officer wears the Glengarry. It is notable that no badges of rank are to be seen. (Courtesy, R. G. Harris)**

and a second to Mesopotamia. After the Russian Revolution the latter went as far north as the Caspian Sea with a view to keeping the revolution out of Persia. The 4th fought in the Dardanelles alongside the 5th; in fact an officer and twenty-five men of the 5th were the last men to evacuate the Gallipoli Peninsula.

The 1st/6th held the Suez Canal in 1914, and this became the setting for a famous anecdote. A British warship was steaming slowly through the canal on a dark night. 'Halt! Who goes there?' challenged a lone Gurkha sentry, undismayed by the sheer bulk of the battleship. It is said that the ship obligingly stopped while an officer was found to explain to the sentry that the warship was entitled to sail through the canal. 'Pass, friend,' shouted the sentry, and the Royal Navy was permitted to carry on with the war. . . . After service in Gallopoli the 6th went on to Mesopotamia and thence to the Caspian Sea, while the 2nd battalion went yet further to south Russia and the Caucasus, and thence to Greece via the Black Sea.

The 1/7th remained as a training unit in India, while the 2nd battalion went via the Suez Canal to Mesopotamia where they had the ill-fortune to be taken at the fall of Kut. They did, however, receive the honour of marching out under arms. Curiously enough a newly raised replacement battalion took part in the recapture of Kut-al-Amara.

The 8th extended yet further the ground covered by the Gurkhas by going to Palestine, while the 2nd battalion went to France, where on 25 September 1914 the battalion lost all but 150 men.

The 9th fought in France and had two battalions in Mesopotamia, and the 10th saw action in Mesopotamia, Suez, and Gallipoli.

Perhaps the easiest way to see the services rendered by the Gurkhas during the First World War would be to read the regimental battle honours given below.

THE BATTLE HONOURS OF THE GURKHA RIFLE REGIMENTS IN THE FIRST WORLD WAR

1st. 'Givenchy, 1914', 'Neuve Chapelle', 'Ypres, 1915', 'St Julien', 'Festubert, 1915', 'Loos', 'France and Flanders, 1914–15', 'Megiddo', 'Sharon', 'Palestine, 1918', 'Tigris, 1916', 'Kut-al-Amara, 1917', 'Baghdad', 'Mesopotamia, 1916–18'.

2nd. 'La Bassee, 1914', 'Festubert, 1914–15', 'Givenchy, 1914', 'Neuve Chapelle', 'Aubers', 'Loos', 'France and Flanders, 1914–15', 'Egypt, 1915', 'Tigris, 1916', 'Kut-al-Amara, 1917', 'Baghdad', 'Mesopotamia, 1916–18', 'Persia, 1918'.

3rd. 'La Bassee, 1914', 'Armentières, 1914', 'Festubert, 1914–15', 'Givenchy, 1914', 'Neuve Chapelle', 'Aubers', 'France and Flanders, 1914–15', 'Egypt, 1915–16', 'Gaza', 'El Mughar', 'Nebi Samwil', 'Jerusalem', 'Tell-Asur', 'Megiddo', 'Sharon', 'Mesopotamia, 1917–18'.

4th. 'Givenchy, 1914', 'Neuve Chapelle', 'Ypres, 1915', 'St Julien', 'Aubers', 'Festubert, 1915', 'France and Flanders, 1914–15', 'Gallipoli, 1915', 'Egypt, 1916', 'Tigris, 1916', 'Kut-al-Amara, 1917', 'Baghdad', 'Mesopotamia, 1916–18'.

5th. 'Helles', 'Krithia', 'Suvla', 'Sari Bair', 'Gallipoli, 1915', 'Suez Canal', 'Egypt, 1915–16', 'Khan Bagdadi', 'Mesopotamia, 1916–18',

6th. 'Helles', 'Krithia', 'Suvla', 'Sari Bair', 'Gallipoli, 1915', 'Suez Canal', 'Egypt, 1916–18', 'Khan Bagdadi', 'Mesopotamia, 1916–18', 'Persia, 1918'.

7th. 'Suez Canal', 'Egypt, 1915', 'Megiddo', 'Sharon', 'Palestine, 1918', 'Shaiba', 'Kut-al-Amara, 1915–17', 'Ctesiphon', 'Defence of Kut-al-Amara', 'Baghdad', 'Sharqat', 'Mesopotamia, 1915–18'.

8th. 'La Bassée, 1914', 'Festubert, 1914–15', 'Givenchy, 1914', 'Neuve Chapelle', 'Aubers', 'France and Flanders, 1914–15', 'Egypt, 1915–16', 'Megiddo', 'Sharon', 'Palestine, 1918', 'Tigris, 1916', 'Kut-al-Amara, 1917', 'Baghdad', 'Mesopotamia, 1916–18',

9th. 'La Bassée, 1914', 'Armentières, 1914', 'Festubert, 1914, 1915', 'Givenchy, 1914', 'Neuve Chapelle', 'Aubers', 'Loos', 'France and Flanders, 1914–15', 'Tigris, 1916', 'Kut-al-Amara, 1917', 'Baghdad', 'Mesopotamia, 1916–18'.

10th. 'Helles', 'Krithia', 'Suvla', 'Sari Bair', 'Gallipoli, 1915', 'Suez Canal', 'Egypt, 1915', 'Sharqat', 'Mesopotamia, 1916–18'.

The years between the two world wars were no peaceful period of rest and tranquillity. While European armies were being demobilized in 1919, all ten Gurkha regiments were engaged on the North-west Frontier of India, as were three battalions of the 11th who, raised for the war, did not

The 3rd Goorkhas leaving Bareilly for Afghanistan, 1878. Despite the source of the sketch this should not be taken as accurate reference. The 3rd did not wear a diced cap, and the white gaiters are suspect, though possible. The officers appear to be wearing khaki helmets. (*Illustrated London News*)

long survive it. In Waziristan in 1919, on the Malabar coast in 1921–2, Waziristan again in 1925 and Burma in 1930–2, there was little time to relax. The face of war was changing. Aircraft and armour and other new weapons had to be assimilated into the traditional methods of frontier warfare in which the Gurkhas so excelled. By the time that the newly joined subalterns of the First World War rejoiced in field rank, command of regiments, or enjoyed their well-earned retirement, the Second World War broke out.

The complexities of this great conflict make it impossible to follow in any detail the activities of the ten regiments of Gurkha Rifles, and only a brief mention can be made of the more important events.

The 1st served in Burma, as did the 2nd, which raised no less than five battalions which saw service in Persia, the Western Desert, North Africa, Italy, Greece, and Malaya.

The 3rd were in Burma and also in Italy, in common with the 4th and 5th, the latter excelling themselves in earning no less than four V.C.s – three in Italy and one in Burma.

The 6th expanded to four battalions of which the 1st, 3rd, and 4th operated in Burma with the famous Chindits, while the 2nd went to Persia, Iraq, and Palestine and finally to Italy.

Of the 7th, the 1st battalion fought throughout in Burma, while the ill-fated 2nd battalion repeated its First World War misfortune when taken prisoner at the fall of Tobruk. A replacement battalion which was raised served in Syria,

Lebanon, and Palestine, training as a special mountain unit. It fought in the Battle of Monte Cassino and was thereafter stationed in Greece.

The 8th served in Italy and Burma, while the 9th were present at Monte Cassino, as well as operating with the Chindits in Burma.

The 10th expanded to four battalions, serving in Syria, Iraq, Italy, Palestine, and, of course, Burma.

Two further regiments which were raised for the duration of the war, the 25th and 26th, were disbanded shortly after peace was declared.

Partition

In 1947 Pakistan and India opted to go their separate ways and the Labour Government of the day, in a gesture of unparalleled irresponsibility, gave India and Pakistan their freedom without adequate arrangements having been made for the protection of minorities. The total count of casualties will never be known, but a reasonable estimate is of the order of two million deaths in Hindu-Moslem conflicts marked by medieval cruelty. At the same time the Indian princes, who had treaties with the British Government guaranteeing their rights and status, were abandoned to their fate.

The division of the subcontinent meant the division of the armed forces. Four of the Gurkha regiments went to the British Army, namely the 2nd, 6th, 7th, and 10th. The remaining regiments joined the new Indian Army. Those regiments who took service with the British were designated the Brigade of Gurkhas on 1 January 1948.

They were soon in action again in Malaya, since which time they have served in Borneo, Sarawak, Brunei, and on the borders of Hong Kong.

New Formations

Since their new status as part of the British Army, the Gurkhas have formed new units designed to make them a self-contained force. These include a short-lived experiment in which, during the emergency in Malaya, the 7th second battalion

A number of cold-weather uniforms displayed by officers of the 5th Goorkha Regiment (Hazara Goorkha Battalion), *c.* 1880. These vary from the full-dress rifle-green tunic faced with black velvet, to the undress rifle-green patrol, and the *poshteen* or Afghan coat: this latter is of goatskin, with the hair inside, and embroidered with yellow silk. All wear the undress forage cap or pillbox. Rank-badges are worn on the collar, and no shoulder-straps are visible. The patrol seems to lack outside pockets, but the edges appear to be braided. There are no pointed cuffs or cuff buttons on these. Overalls and breeches have wide black lace stripes. Note the long black gaiters worn by the seated officer in patrol; and the half-Wellingtons with swan-neck spurs of the adjutant on the right. The belts are black with silver mounts, the sword-knots black, and the scabbards leather with steel mounts. Note, that at this early date the binocular case on the dress pouch-belt was a dummy – the records of Messrs Ranken, military tailors, read: 'Binocular Case – Black patent leather, very small and flat (not to hold glasses).'

was recognized as 102 Field Regiment Royal Artillery (7th Gurkha Rifles).

In 1961 men from the 7th and 10th were trained as parachutists, these forming the nucleus of the Gurkha Independent Parachute Company which was formed the following year when trouble broke out with Indonesia. For a time these men trained and worked with the Border Scouts, a police unit formed to cover the border area between Sarawak, Sabah, and Indonesia. Later the unit was trained on the lines of the S.A.S.

In 1948 an Engineer Field Squadron was raised from Gurkha infantrymen, attached to the Royal Engineers, and given the number 67. Two years later a second squadron was formed with the number 68, and in the following year Regimental Headquarters of the 50th Field Engineer Regiment was formed in Hong Kong. In 1958 the regiment became an integral part of the Gurkha Brigade, with the title Gurkha Engineers, in 1960.

No infantry brigade would be complete without adequate signal facilities and so in 1948 training was commenced to form a new Gurkha Independent Signal Squadron. By 1954 the unit had increased in size and was restyled the Gurkha Signals.

The Gurkha Transport Regiment originated in two companies formed in Malaya in July 1958.

The first title was the Gurkha Army Service Corps, but this was changed in 1965 to the Gurkha Transport Regiment. Wherever Gurkhas are found their transport unit is present.

The Gurkha Military Police were formed in 1955 as part of the Brigade of Gurkhas, and affiliated to the Corps of Military Police. In 1966 they were amalgamated with the Dog Company, a unit raised to guard installations. Gurkha personnel were trained in dog-handling and established as 5 (Gurkha) Dog Company in 1963. Amalgamated in 1966 with the other Gurkha military police units under the title of 5 Gurkha Dog Company, the unit was finally disbanded in 1969.

PROGRESSIVE TITLE CHANGES OF THE GURKHA REGIMENTS

1st King George V's Own Gurkha Rifles (the Malaun Regiment)

1815 1st Nasiri Battalion; 1823 5th, 6th, or 1st Nasiri Local Battalion; 1826 4th, or Nasiri Local Battalion; 1843 4th or Nasiri (Rifle Battalion); 1850 66th or Goorkha Regiment, Bengal Native Infantry; 1858 66th or Goorkha Light Infantry Regiment, Bengal Native Infantry; 1861 11th Regiment of Bengal Native Infantry; 1861 1st Goorkha Regiment (Light Infantry); 1886 1st Goorkha Regiment (Light Infantry); 1891 1st Gurkha (Rifle) Regiment; 1901 1st Gurkha Rifles; 1903 1st Gurkha Rifles (the Malaun

Regiment); 1906 1st Prince of Wales Own Gurkha Rifles; 1910 1st King George's Own Gurkha Rifles (The Malaun Regiment); 1937 1st King George V's Own Gurkha Rifles (the Malaun Regiment); 1947 left the British service.

2nd King Edward VII's Own Goorkhas (the Sirmoor Rifles)

1815 Sirmoor Battalion; 1823 8th (or Sirmoor) Local Battalion; 1826 6th (or Sirmoor) Local Battalion; 1850 Sirmoor Battalion; 1858 Sirmoor Rifle Regiment; 1861 17th Regiment of Bengal Native Infantry; 1861 2nd Goorkha Regiment; 1864 2nd Goorkha (the Sirmoor Rifles) Regiment; 1876 2nd (Prince of Wales's Own) Goorkha Regiment (the Sirmoor Rifles); 1886 2nd (the Prince of Wales's Own) Goorkha Regiment (The Sirmoor Rifles); 1891 2nd (the Prince of Wales's own) Gurkha (Rifles) Regiment (the Sirmoor Rifles); 1901 2nd (the Prince of Wales's Own) Gurkha Rifles (the Sirmoor Rifles); 1 Jan. 1906 2nd King Edward's Own Gurkha Rifles (the Sirmoor Rifles), 1936 2nd King Edward VII's Own Goorkhas (the Sirmoor Rifles); 1947 to British Army.

3rd Queen Alexandra's Own Gurkha Rifles

1815 Kumaon Battalion; 1816 Kumaon Provincial Battalion; 1823 9th (or Kumaon) Local Battalion; 1826 7th (or Kumaon) Local Battalion; 1860 Kumaon Battalion; 1861 18th Regiment of Bengal Native Infantry; 1861 3rd Goorkha Regiment; 1864 3rd (the Kumaon) Goorkha Regiment; 1887 3rd Goorkha Regiment; 1891 3rd Goorkha (Rifle) Regiment; 1901 3rd Gurkha Rifles; 1907 3rd The Queen's Own Gurkha Rifles; 1908 3rd Queen Alexandra's Own Gurkha Rifles; 1947 left the British service.

4th Prince of Wales's Own Gurkha Rifles

1857 Extra Goorhka Regiment; 1861 19th Regiment of Bengal Native Infantry; 1861 4th Goorkha Regiment; 1891 4th Gurkha (Rifle) Regiment; 1901 4th Gurkha Rifles; 1924 4th Prince of Wales's Own Gurkha Rifles; 1947 left the British service.

5th Royal Gurkha Rifles (Frontier Force)

1858 25th Punjab Infantry, or Hazara Goorkha Battalion; 1861 7th Regiment of Infantry (or Hazara Goorkha Battalion), Punjab Irregular Force; 1861 5th Goorkha Regiment, or Hazara Goorkha Battalion; 1886 5th Goorkha Regiment, the Hazara Goorkha Battalion; 1887 5th Goorkha Regiment; 1891 5th Gurkha (Rifle) Regiment; 1901 5th Gurkha Rifles; 1903 5th Gurkha Rifles (Frontier Force); 1923 5th Royal Gurkha Rifles (Frontier Force); 1947 left the British service.

6th Queen Elizabeth's Own Gurkha Rifles

1817 Cuttack Legion; 1823 Rangpur Light Infantry Battalion; 1826 8th (or Rangpur) Local Light Infantry Battalion; 1828 8th (or Assam) Local Light Infantry Battalion; 1844 1st Assam Light Infantry; 1861 46th Regiment of Bengal Native Infantry; 1861 42nd Regiment of Bengal Native Infantry; 1864 42nd (Assam) Regiment of Bengal Native (Light) Infantry; 1885 42nd (Assam) Regiment of Bengal (Light) Infantry; 1886 42nd Regiment Goorkha Light Infantry; 1889 42nd (Goorkha) Regiment of Bengal (Light) Infantry; 1891 42nd Gurkha (Rifle) Regiment of Bengal Infantry; 1901 42nd Gurkha Rifles; 1903 6th Gurkha Rifles; 1947 to British Army; 1959 6th Queen Elizabeth's Own Gurkha Rifles.

7th Duke of Edinburgh's Own Gurkha Rifles

1902 8th Gurkha Rifles; 1903 2nd Battalion, 10th Gurkha Rifles; 1907 7th Gurkha Rifles; 1947 to British Army; 1 Jan. 1959 7th Duke of Edinburgh's Own Gurkha Rifles.

8th Gurkha Rifles

1824 16th or Sylhet Local Battalion; 1826 11th or Sylhet Local (Light) Infantry Battalion; 1861 48th Regiment of Bengal Native Infantry; 1861 44th Regiment of Bengal Native Infantry; 1864 44th (Sylhet) Regiment of Bengal Native (Light) Infantry; 1885 44th (Sylhet) Regiment of Bengal (Light) Infantry; 1886 44th Regiment, Goorkha (Light) Infantry; 1889 44th (Goorkha) Regiment of Bengal (Light) Infantry; 1891 44th Gurkha (Rifle) Regiment of Bengal Infantry; 1901 44th Gurkha Rifles; 1903 8th Gurkha Rifles; 1907 became the 1st Battalion. 2nd Battalion, raised at Gauhati: 1835 Assam Sebundy Corps; 1839 Lower Assam Sebundy Corps; 1839 1st Assam Sebundy Corps; 1844 2nd Assam Light infantry; 1861 47th Regiment of Bengal Native Infantry; 1861 43rd Regiment of Bengal Native Infantry; 1884 43rd (Assam) Regiment of Bengal Native (Light) Infantry; 1865 43rd (Assam) Regiment of Bengal (Light) Infantry; 1886 43rd Regiment Goorka Light Infantry; 1889 43rd (Goorkha) Regiment of Bengal (Light) Infantry; 1891 43rd Gurkha (Rifle) Regiment of Bengal Infantry; 1901 43rd Gurkha Rifles; 1903 7th Gurkha Rifles; 1907 became the 2nd Battalion, 8th Gurkha Rifles; 1947 left the British service.

9th Gurkha Rifles

1817 Fatehgarh Levy; 1819 Manipuri Levy; 1823 1st Battalion, 32nd Regiment of Bengal Native Infantry; 1824 63rd Regiment of Bengal Native Infantry; 1861 9th Regiment of Bengal Native Infantry;

1885 9th Regiment of Bengal Infantry; 1894 9th (Gurkha Rifles) Regiment of Bengal Infantry; 1901 9th Gurkha Rifles; 1947 left the British service.

10th Princess Mary's Own Gurkha Rifles

1890 1st Regiment of Burma Infantry; 1891 10th Regiment (1st Burma Battalion) of Madras Infantry; 1892 10th Regiment (1st Burma Rifles) Madras Infantry; 1895 10th Regiment (1st Burma Gurkha Rifles) Madras Infantry; 1901 10th Gurkha Rifles; 1947 to British Army; 1949 10th Princess Mary's Own Gurkha Rifles.

Notes on Uniforms

The colour plates in this book have been prepared by reference to surviving prints, sketches, paintings, photographs, written descriptions, and uniform regulations; many of the illustrations from which they have been drawn are reproduced in the body of the text. While space forbids the quotation of all relevant uniform regulations concerning the dress of British officers of Gurkha units, and while the paucity of available documentation on many aspects of other ranks' dress must be admitted, the author nevertheless trusts that the following notes on certain aspects of these uniforms may be helpful.

1815–1882

Since the original formations which were later to develop into the Gurkha regiments were not part of the Regular Army at the time of raising, some

variation between their dress and that of the Regulars is not surprising, and unfortunately there is very little detail available. There are, however, a few regulations which are to be found assembled in Bengal Military Regulations, 1817, which were supposed to be in force at that date, and which were 'inserted for the information, and guidance of those officers of the Company's Army, to whom they are applicable'. Thus item 187 gives the uniform of four Provincial battalions as red with green facings. This probably applied at least to the Kumaon Provincial Battalion raised in 1816. As a general guide-line, item 115 specified that the uniform of Provincial battalions was 'to correspond as nearly as possible with the uniform of the regular Native Corps', according to a proclamation of the Governor-General of 25 August and 3 October 1803. A general order by the Governor-General of 8 December 1809 stated that the uniform of Hill Rangers was 'to remain, as at present, with green facings, white buttons and lace'. The Regular Bengal line infantry was to wear red, with yellow facings, and lace, striped red, blue, and white.

European officers and N.C.O.s posted to Native regiments were to wear round black hats, 'the ornaments for the hats to be left to the Commanding Officer of the Regiment; the Buttons to be the lion Button, bearing the number of the Regiment'. The lion was the heraldic beast of the Honourable East India Company. Officers of light companies were to have 'suitable wings to their jackets' (95). Native commissioned officers were to wear white

The 5th Goorkha Regiment in summer dress, 1882. This hot-weather uniform consists of a khaki drill jacket and dark trousers. Possibly the khaki was not the modern version, for in the 2nd the so-called khaki was a 'slatey grey', and was adopted in 1882 in lieu of the previously worn 'black serge'. The Kilmarnock has the crossed kukri badge; N.C.O. chevrons are black. The Gurkha officers wear their dress shoulder-belts, and their sword-belts under their jackets. Note the rolled haversack on the nearest figure. (National Army Museum)

1 Gurkha Sepoy, 1815
2 Sepoy, Cuttack Legion (later 6th
  Gurkha Rifles), 1817
3 Native officer, 1st Nasiri Battalion
  (later 1st Gurkha Rifles), 1820

1

2

3

MICHAEL ROFFE

A

1 Sepoy, Sirmoor Battalion (later 2nd
  Gurkha Rifles), 1840s
2 British officer, Nasiri Battalion
  (later 1st Gurkha Rifles), 1840s
3 Sepoy, 5th Goorkha Regiment, 1865

B

1 **Subadar-Major and Honorary Lieutenant, 3rd Goorkha Regiment, 1870**

2 **Rifleman, 3rd Goorkha Regiment, 1870**

3 **Subadar-Major, 44th (Sylhet) Regiment, Bengal Native (Light) Infantry, c. 1870**

1 Sepoy, 1st Goorkha Regiment, 1880
2 Sepoy, 5th Goorkha Regiment, 1886
3 Lance-Naik, 2nd Goorkha Regiment, 1889

D

1 Rifleman, 2nd Gurkha Rifles, *c.* 1895
2 Jemadar, 2nd Gurkha Rifles, with
  Queen's Truncheon, *c.* 1895
3 British officer, 2nd Gurkha Rifles,
  c. 1898

1

2

3

1 British officer, 2nd Gurkha Rifles,
  c. 1902
2 Subadar-Major, 1907
3 Bugler, 6th Gurkha Rifles, 1912

F

MICHAEL ROFFE

1 **Rifleman, 1914**
2 **Bugle-Major, 8th Gurkha Rifles,**
   c. 1930
3 **Rifleman, c. 1935**

1 Havildar, 4th Indian Division,
  Italy, 1944
2 British officer, 1950s
3 Rifleman, Borneo, *c.* 1960

ntaloons and half-boots, and their swords and
:lts to be the same as those of British officers,
ith the number only upon the plate (97).

The 'kummerbund (waist sash worn by Native
her ranks) is to be of blue linen and six inches
breadth to be girt round the loins and fastened
ehind, in whatever manner may be found most
onvenient, the Cross to be of white linen.' Native
ommissioned officers and havildars (sergeants)
ore sashes. This was confirmed by an order of
e G.O.C.C. in November 1809.

The standard nether wear for naiks (corporals)
nd sepoys were 'Jangheas' or shorts, white with
zigzag border of black or dark blue. An order
ad permitted havildars to wear pantaloons
istead of the jangheas – entirely at their own
equest (and, of course, expense).

The turban was made more bearable by an
rder of 1806: 'The frame of the turban directed
o be worn by the Native Infantry of the Army
'y General Order, dated the 26th July, 1805, is
o be made of rattan instead of iron work, when-
ver it is necessary to make new turbans; and the
air of the men is to be worn turned up and
astened in a knot on the crown of the head, as
efore, instead of being cut and turned down
oose as practised by some Corps, and of which
he Commander-in-Chief disapproves.'

Officers of flank companies, as in the British
ervice were to wear sabres of an approved regimental pattern (123), and all infantry officers
when on duty were to wear gorgets, gilt, engraved
with the arms of the Honourable East India
Company, and suspended by ribbons of the colour
of the regimental facings (September 1813).

The wearing, or not, as the case may be, of
pantaloons, took up an inordinate amount of
wording. There appeared to be no uniformity of
concept among the regiments, a grave matter
disturbing to the C.-in-C. No pressure to adopt
he pantaloon was to be applied to the men,
especially as they were to have the privilege of
paying for them from their own pockets. But 'when
in compliance with the general desire of a Corps
it may be resolved to wear Pantaloons such shall
be in the shape of Trowsers, of a moderate width,
and reaching fully down to the ancle, but never
made tight to fit the limbs, which besides imposing
constraint upon the Sepoy, His Excellency has

Painting by A. C. Lovett of
a soldier of the 4th
Goorkha Regiment in 1885.
Lovett illustrated Major
G. F. MacMunn's famous
Armies of India, published
in 1911. Note long
triangular-bladed bayonet,
white linen haversack,
linen waterbottle sling, and
kukri frog. The long gaiters
were sometimes worn by
British officers. (National
Army Museum)

had opportunities of observing, is particularly un-
favourable to the Appearance of the Corps. Naiks
and Sepoys are to wear only their trowsers,
Havildars to be distinguished by the addition of
gaiters.' (167). 'Pantaloons are only to be worn
between the 1st October and the 1st April
annually', said No. 168, but this was speedily
altered by an order of a month later, June 1813,
extending the use of pantaloons throughout the
year.

It is unfortunate that no mention is made of any
Rifle Corps, and so details of the early rifle
uniform are missing.

The 1st Nasiri Battalion would apparently have
worn the scarlet, and the historian of the 2nd,
Colonel L. Shakespeare, says that not until 1816
did the Sirmoor Battalion have leisure to provide
itself with anything like a uniform. This took the
form of a dark green coatee, black facings and
wings, five rows of black and white braid on the
breast, and their own black native head-dress. In
the 1820s the previously worn white trousers were
replaced by blue drill, and the lace on the coatee
changed to red. A shako was now taken into
(unpopular) use, and the buglers were put into

25

red coatees with green facings. The arms were the 'Brown Bess' and bayonet and the kukri. In the early 1830s the facings were changed to black and the musket replaced by a 'fusil'. In 1849 the regiment was taken on to the Regular establishment, and rearmed with the two-grooved Brunswick rifle. The uniform was now all rifle green; the white trousers and the black and white or red lace all disappeared.

There seems to be little available to show the uniform of British officers at this period. However, it seems reasonable to assume that they followed closely the costume worn by British Rifle officers, wearing the braided dolman, though possibly the astrakhan-edged pelisse might not have appeared in the tropics. But the temperature even in summer can fall somewhat low in hill stations such as Dehra Dun, so it may have been adopted, as was done in the Madras Army.

The earliest detailed information on the dress of officers of Local Hill Corps is given in an adjutant-general's circular of 9 January 1829. These instructions are repeated exactly in the Bengal Army Regulations of 1841:

ORDERS RELATIVE TO THE UNIFORM AND APPOINTMENTS OF THE ARMY, 1841

The dress uniform is to be worn at divine service, at levees, public field days, general inspections, funeral parties, grand guard mounting, general, district, and garrison courts martial, public parties, places of public resort, and visits of ceremony.

The undress is for general use, and to be worn on all occasions not specified above.

The frock-coat is only intended to be worn on certain duties off parade; viz. inspection of barracks and hospitals, courts of inquiry, committees, private inspection parades, working parties, fatigue duties, and on the march.

The sash and undress sword-belt are always to be worn with the frock-coat when on duty.

The shell-jacket is always to be hooked or buttoned when worn on duty; when used as an undress, on occasions not connected with duty, it may be left open; but the waistcoat worn with it must be of the authorized pattern.

A white linen uniform jacket, with ten small regimental buttons, set on by twos in front and two on the collar, may be worn when the men are permitted to wear their white dress, but this indulgence is restricted to ordinary duties and parades.

Ensigns, until finally posted, are only required to provide themselves with the undress uniform of the regiment with which they may be doing duty.

LOCAL HILL CORPS AND LIGHT INFANTRY BATTALIONS

DRESS

Jacket – Dark green cloth, hussar style; Prussian collar, full three inches deep, ornament with black mohair braid; collar and cuffs of regimental facings; single-breasted, with three rows of ball-buttons, and Russia braid loops, very close together all the way down the front; pointed cuffs, three inches deep at the point, ornamented with braid; figured on the sleeves, side seams, welts, and hips; no wings or epaulettes are worn.
Cap – Black beaver, bell-shaped, seven inches and a half deep; black, sunk glazed top, eleven

The Goorkhas, 1885. It is difficult to be more specific about this group. The uniform pattern is correct, but the only regiment in which Gurkha officers wore the tunic was the 2nd, who also wore the red/black diced cap-band, absent here. The 1st also adopted red facings, as here, but their badge had the kukri blades downwards. The officer's white helmet also poses a puzzle at this date. For all its inconsistencies, it is a pleasing and spirited picture. (Author's collection)

inches in diameter; a black silk band round the top, two inches and three quarters wide; a patent leather band round the bottom, one inch wide; a black lace double circle in the centre (*of the front*), communicating by a black bullion loop and button to a bullion rosette at the top; black lines and acorn tassels; bronzed scales and lions' heads, black stamped peak.

Tuft – A round black ball (or tuft) to be worn, in place of a feather.

Trousers – Dark green, with a double stripe of black Russia braid down the outward seam.

Boots were described as 'ankle', and the regulation infantry sabre was specified. The black leather scabbard had steel mounts and a plain black leather sword-knot was worn. A black leather waist-belt with a snake fastening was described; the black pouch-belt was ornamented with an engraved plate and a lion's head, a whistle and a chain. The pouch-flap bore a bugle device. A black silk net sash was worn.

For undress wear a jacket 'similar to dress, only with a less proportion of trimming' was specified, with straight-cut, rather loose dark green trousers without ornament of any kind, and a 'plain light shako, with an oilskin cover'. All other items were as for full dress. A forage cap was described, of 'plain green cloth welted with the colour of the facings; a black leather peak, and a band of black silk lace or mohair two inches broad, and a black silk knob at the top'. Commanding officers, seconds in command, and adjutants were also to wear plain black patent leather sabretaches on three slings from the waist-belt, and steel screw spurs; their scabbards were of steel. Note that at this date all Gurkha regiments dressed in green wore black facings and lace.

The terrible conditions encountered in the Crimean War had demonstrated the impractical aspects of contemporary British military costume in most forceful manner, and uniforms were in process of drastic alteration when the great Mutiny of the Bengal Army exploded in 1857. The change had already started in the British Army, and in January 1857 the General Officer Commanding-in-Chief in India issued an order applicable to all presidency armies (those of Madras, Bengal, and Bombay) authorizing '*tunics* being worn by all officers who are at present without dress coatees

. . . to be of the patterns prescribed for the royal army in the dress regulations issued from Horse Guards'. (Note that 'Horse Guards' refers to the headquarters of the British Army housed in the building of that name in Whitehall, London, and not to the regiment of that name.)

In June 1858 infantry officers were peremptorily ordered to 'provide themselves with new pattern uniforms as laid down in HM regulations at once'. Evidently little notice had been taken of the previous order. In 1859 official sanction was accorded to the already existing practice: 'All regimental officers are to provide themselves with light wicker or felt helmets of the description established for staff officers . . . to be worn on all occasions on which the forage cap covered is now worn.'

Troubled times are not conducive to uniform clothing, and the fearful sartorial follies of irregular troops tended to exercise a baneful influence. The newly raised 25th Punjab Infantry or Hazara Goorkha was an example to all. The officers appeared in helmets with cocks'-feather plumes, a green silk puggree intertwined with chain, loose light green frogged tunics, a shield, and a red silk sash. The last two items proved too much for the commander of the Punjab Irregular Force, Brigadier Neville Chamberlain, and he ordered their abolition.

In January 1858 the G.O.C.-in-C. found it necessary to issue a general 'raspberry' about slackness in general and the absence of shakos in particular. The widespread introduction of informal khaki clothing had proved so popular that all were loath to return to more formal attire. Khaki was blamed for 'the introduction of slovenly habits at variance with the proverbial correct and neat appearance of the officers and soldiers of the British Army'.

After the Mutiny many changes from the old costume were introduced. Of these the earliest regulations to hand are those of the Punjab Frontier Force for 1865, which force included the 5th Goorkha Battalion with their black facings. These regulations describe a costume which includes the hussar type of braided tunic to be seen in later photographs, and a grey felt helmet, which Colonel Shakespeare states was adopted in the 2nd in 1859. The description is as follows: 'Drab felt, low and well-shaped, with silver bars, binding and spike. Chin-straps of silver chain lined with drab patent leather, fastening on each side to a lion's head. A silver device in front of the helmet similar to the regimental breastplate.' No turban or puggree was worn in dress uniform. The black steel-mounted sword scabbard is described as 'donkey skin'. The undress coat is described as 'single-breasted, the collar rounded in front, to fasten with hooks and eyes down to the waist, edged all round with drab braid three-quarters inch wide. The sleeve regulation size, ornamented with drab [black for 5th?] Austrian knot. This coat can be lined with black lamb's wool for winter wear when the Privates wear the Posteen, or the Posteen itself can be worn by officers as well as men.' This can be seen in the group of officers, c. 1880.

The turban or puggree was never popular with the Gurkhas. The 2nd adopted it for a time, and the regimental history states that permission was obtained to wear a khaki puggree in service dress in lieu of the khaki-covered Kilmarnock, the regiment first parading in this innovation on 3 January 1898.

*   *   *

UNIFORM OF BRITISH OFFICERS SERVING WITH REGIMENTS DRESSED IN GREEN, BENGAL ARMY, 1882

DISTINCTIONS OF RANK

Field officers – Collar laced all round with black lace, figured braiding within the lace; sleeve ornament, lace and figured braiding eleven inches deep.

Captains – Collar laced round the top with black lace, with figured braiding below the lace; sleeve ornament, knot of square cord with figured braiding eight inches deep.

Lieutenants – Collar laced round the top with black lace and plain edging of braid; sleeve ornament, knot of square cord and braid seven inches deep.

Tunic – Rifle green, with collar and cuffs of regimental facings, single-breasted; the collar rounded in front; on each side of the breast, five loops of black square cord, with netted caps and drops, fastening with worked olivets, the top loop eight inches long, the bottom four inches; shoulder-straps of Hussar pattern in black. Badges of rank in bronze on shoulder-straps.

Note: Badges of rank, which had been worn on the collar from 1857 to 1880, were as follows:

Colonel	Crown and two stars below
Lieutenant-Colonel	Crown and one star below
Major	Crown
Captain	Two stars
Lieutenant	One star
Second Lieutenant	No badges

The tunic edged all round (except the collar) with black square cord. On the back seams a single cord, forming three eyes at the top, passing under a netted button at the waist, below which it is doubled and terminating in a knot at the bottom of the skirt. The skirt, nine inches deep for an officer five feet nine inches in height, with the variation of an eighth of an inch for every inch of difference in height, lined with black and rounded in front.

Trousers – Rifle-green cloth, with a braid of black mohair two inches wide down the outward seam.
Boots – Wellington or ankle.
Spurs – Steel, crane-neck, two inches long.
Pantaloons – Rifle-green cloth, with outward seam braid as in trousers.
Scabbard – Steel (*brass for field officers*).
Sword-knot – Black leather strap and acorn.
Sword-belt – Black patent leather, one and a half inches wide, with slings one inch wide, silver snake clasp, and mountings; to be worn under the tunic.
Sword – Same as prescribed for officers dressed in red, except that the hilt is of steel, and the device is a crown and bugle.
Sabretache – Black leather, perfectly plain without device or badge, with black leather slings. (*This item was abolished in 1884.*)
Pouch – Black leather, with a silver bugle on the flap. The 2nd Prince of Wales's Own Sirmoor Rifles has a special bronze badge of ostrich feathers.
Pouch-belt – Black patent leather, three inches wide, with silver regimental plate, whistle and chain. In the 2nd Goorkhas the plate is of bronze.
Gloves – Black leather.
Patrol Jacket – Rifle-green cloth, of sufficient length to just clear the saddle when mounted, with collar and cuffs of regimental facing and rounded off in

Band of the 1st Battalion, 5th Goorkha Regiment, 1888. The rifle-green uniform has black facings and lace and black puttees and equipment. Note the European bandmaster in civilian costume – European bandmasters were still to be seen in some Gurkha units until at least 1939. The instrument on the extreme right was not carried on the line of march. (National Army Museum)

front; one-inch mohair braid all round and up open slits at side; five double drop loops with eyes in centre, $\frac{3}{4}$ inch flat plait up the front; top loop eight and a half inches, and bottom loop six inches long. One row of knitted olivets. The sleeve will be braided with one inch mohair braid, six inches high, with a tracing of mohair braid above and below, forming three eyes at the upper and three eyes at the lower point. Crow's-feet of flat plait at top and bottom of curved side seams, with two eyes at equal distances, lower eyes one inch apart, hooks and eyes up front to neck, stand-up collar, with one inch mohair braid round the upper edge. Pockets fitted with flap in and out. Shoulder-straps and badges of rank as with tunic.

Forage Cap – Rifle-green cloth, plain black silk band, black button and braid on top, black leather chin-strap.

Active Service and Peace Manoeuvre Cap – Green cloth of special pattern, ornamented in front with a silver bugle placed on a scarlet cord boss for the 2nd Goorkhas, and on black cord boss for other regiments. (*An amendment of July 1884 ordered the bugle in the 2nd to be of bronze, not silver.*)

Helmet and Spike – Same as prescribed for officers dressed in red, but covered with rifle-green cloth, with a bronze curb chain chin-strap and spike.

Helmets – A cork helmet, covered with cloth and bound about with a puggree, will be the universal day-time dress for all (*British*) arms.

The helmet is covered with white cloth except where otherwise specified, in six seams, bound with buff leather at the bottom; and above the peak and going round the helmet a buff leather band one inch wide, stitched top and bottom. The headpiece is to be let in with zigzag ventilation, giltside hooks, gilt hook near top on right side to fasten up chin-strap; gilt curb chain chin-strap, the links $\frac{5}{8}$ of an inch wide, the strap lined with white leather. At top of helmet a gilt collet rivetted on to a gilt collar, $\frac{3}{8}$th of an inch wide, to receive spike or ball and cup, and base.

A zinc button covered with white cloth is inserted when the spike, or ball and cup, is not used.

White muslin puggrees are worn universally, unless otherwise directed. (Section VI directed that the spike be worn in – Review order, Marching order, Field Day order.)

Puggree – Regimental pattern and colour.

NATIVE OFFICERS

Coat – Rifle-green Zouave jacket with regimental facings, laced with $\frac{1}{2}$ inch black lace round the collar and down the front. Black worsted cord on the shoulders, buttons regimental pattern, eight on the front, one on each shoulder, three on each cuff. Cuffs slashed with three vandykes formed

29

with black lace. Distinctive badges – *kookries* instead of swords on the collar according to rank.* (Subadars – crossed kookries, Jemadar – single kookrie.)

Forage Cap – Kilmarnock except in the 42nd and 43rd Native Infantry, who wear turbans and glengarries respectively.† The number is worn by the 44th Native Infantry.

Paijamahs – Green serge without piping.

Swords, Scabbard, and Belt – As for British officers.

Sword-knot – Black leather.

Pouch and Pouch-belt – As for British officers.

Boots – Regimental pattern.

These regulations are the last to give the scarlet uniform for the 1st Goorkha Regiment (*Light Infantry – late 66th or Goorkha Light Infantry Regiment*).

UNIFORM OF OFFICERS SERVING WITH NATIVE INFANTRY REGIMENTS OF THE BENGAL ARMY DRESSED IN RED

Tunic – Scarlet cloth, single-breasted, eight buttons in front at equal distances, with a fly one and three quarters wide, thus buttoning well over, collar and cuffs of the regimental facing; the collar rounded

This interesting picture shows the colour party of the 2nd escorting the famous silver truncheon presented by Queen Victoria. Note the fairly tight breeches. The Gurkha officer carrying the truncheon has the rank insignia of a jemadar on his collar, and those on the left and right the crossed kukris of subadars. The havildar's stripes are not visible in this picture. (National Army Museum)

* The 2nd Goorkhas wear a tunic, according to an amendment of July 1884.
† The 2nd Goorkhas wear a diced border and a bronze badge of ostrich feathers.

in front; the cuffs pointed; for Lieutenants, laced with one bar of gold lace, half an inch wide, up to a point, seven and a half inches in height; traced outside with gold Russia braid, finishing with an Austrian knot at top making it nine and a half inches high, and showing a light of $\frac{3}{16}$ of an inch of scarlet cloth between the lace and the braid, also traced inside with gold Russia braid finishing down the cuff with crow's-foot and eye, showing light of $\frac{3}{16}$ of an inch of the facing cloth between the lace and the braid. Captains to have two bars of lace showing a $\frac{1}{4}$ inch light of the facing cloth between each, the top bar coming to a point 8 inches high, traced and finished at top and bottom of the lace bars as the Lieutenant's, the top tracing and knot extending 10 inches high. Majors with round eyes on top of the lace showing $\frac{3}{16}$ of scarlet cloth between the lace and the eyes. Colonels and Lieutenant-Colonels have the eyes also below the lower bar of lace, showing $\frac{3}{16}$ of the facing cloth between the braid and the lace; the skirt ten inches deep for an officer five feet nine inches in height, with a variation of $\frac{1}{8}$ inch longer or shorter for every inch difference in height of the wearer; two plaits on skirt behind edged white, with two buttons at waist; the skirts closed behind; the collar and front of coat edged with white a quarter inch wide; the skirts lined with white, shoulder-straps universal pattern, twisted gold cord, lined with scarlet; badges of rank in silver on shoulder-straps; the collar not to exceed two inches high, laced round top with gold lace and gold braid on the collar seam. (Gold-braided eyes inside the lace for Field Officers only; size of eyes $\frac{1}{2}$ inch exterior measurement, $\frac{1}{16}$ inch apart.)

Lace – Gold, half an inch wide, vellum pattern.

Buttons – Gilt, of uniform size, except on the shoulder, which is to be small.

Trousers – Blue cloth, with a scarlet welt down the outward seam, quarter inch broad.

Boots – Wellington or ankle.

Spurs – For field officers, yellow metal with crane necks, two inches long; for other officers, steel of similar pattern.

Pantaloons – Blue cloth with same scarlet welt as trousers, to be worn with the high boots.

Helmet – As in Section VI, with puggree of regimental pattern, the spike to be worn as therein directed.

Colonel Begbie, 2nd Gurkha Regiment: this clear portrait shows in detail the dress uniform of an officer at the turn of the century. Note bronze mounts on the pouch-belt, and the peculiar ram's-head distinction. The Prince of Wales's plumes were adopted when Edward, Prince of Wales, later King Edward VII, became Colonel-in-Chief of the regiment in 1876. (National Army Museum)

The 1st Goorkha Light Infantry wear a badge in gilt metal of crossed kukries, edges downward, the numeral of the regiment in the upper angle, and a bugle in the lower.

Sword – As described.

Scabbard – For field officers, brass; for all other officers, steel.

Sword-knot – Brown leather.

Sword-belt – Of brown leather, one inch and a half wide, with slings and flap and a gilt hook; the sword when hooked up to rest upon the flap, the edge to the rear and the back to the front, to be worn over the tunic and under the patrol jacket.

Sabretache – Brown leather with brown leather slings – perfectly plain without a device or badge.

Waist-plate – A round gilt clasp, having on the centrepiece the number of the regiment, surmounted by a crown, both in silver, and on the outer circle a gilt wreath.

Sash – Crimson silk net, with fringe ends, united by a crimson runner. Worn diagonally over the

left shoulder, and over the sword-belt, the ends of the fringe not to hang below the bottom of the coat. The sash is to be worn in review order whether in cloth or summer clothing, and with the scarlet patrol jacket in marching or field day order; also by the orderly officer.

Gloves – White buckskin leather.

Puggree – Regimental pattern, of the colour of the head-dress worn by the regiment.

Forage Cap – Blue cloth, green for Light Infantry, straight up, three inches high with black patent leather drooping peak and chin strap. Peaks ornamented with half inch full gold embroidery, band of black silk oakleaf lace, with the regimental number in gold embroidery, one inch and a half high, placed on the band in front, black button and trimming on top. Blue cloth* (field officers gold French braid) welt round crown. Royal regiments wear scarlet bands $1\frac{1}{2}$ inches wide.

Active Service and Peace Manoeuvre Cap – Blue glengarry bound an inch wide with black silk riband, with riband ends $1\frac{3}{8}$ inches wide. Black silk cockade on left side, numbers or badges to be worn on the cockade, with a scarlet edging. *Tuft* – Blue, except in Light Infantry, who wear green, and Royal regiments, who wear scarlet. (*This refers to the spherical 'tourie' on top of the cap.*)

Patrol Jacket – Scarlet serge as in Section I.

Section I – Patrol jackets, except those otherwise specified, will be made according to the following description:

Blue cloth, twenty-eight inches long from the bottom of the collar behind, for an officer five feet nine inches in height, with a proportionate variation for any difference in height, rounded in front, and edged with inch black mohair braid all round and up the openings at the sides. On each side in front, four double drop loops of $\frac{1}{4}$ inch flat plait, with eyes in the centre of each loop, the top loop reaching to the sleeve seams, and the bottom ones four inches long; four netted olivets on the right side, to fasten through the loops on the left. On each sleeve, an Austrian knot of flat plait seven inches high from the bottom of the cuff. Double flat plait on each back seam, with crow's-foot at top and bottom, and two double eyes at equal distances. Pockets fitted with flaps in and out. Hooks and eyes in front. Shoulder-straps of blue

* This would be green for light infantry.

31

cloth edged, except at the base, with half inch black mohair braid, with black netted button at top. Badges of rank in gold on shoulder-straps.

Officers of line regiments in India wearing red are not obliged to provide themselves with blue patrol jackets, but will wear the scarlet patrol jacket instead.

Forage Cap – The 1st Goorkha Light Infantry wear a badge in gold embroidery, same device as on helmet.

Pouch-belt of the 3rd Gurkha Rifles, black with silver mounts. Note the form of the crown and the method of intertwining the battle honours with a laurel wreath. (National Army Museum)

NATIVE OFFICERS

Coat – Zouave jackets, scarlet cloth, facings according to the regiment, piped all round with white cloth, laced under the collar and down the front with ¾ inch gold lace, eight buttons down the front, one on the shoulder, scarlet worsted shoulder-cord, slashed cuffs, three buttons on each cuff, three vandykes formed with gold lace.

Distinctive Badges on Collars – Subadars – crossed gold swords; Jemadars – single swords. Native officers in 1st Goorkha Light Infantry wear kookries as collar-badges instead of swords.

Paijamahs – Black serge, with a piping down the side of ¾ inch scarlet lace. Scarlet piping for the 1st Goorkha Light Infantry.

Sword-knot and belt – Brown leather as for British officers.

Sword – As for British officers.

Sash – As for British officers.

Turban – Regimental pattern.

Boots – Regimental pattern.

The Regulations published in 1899 give somewhat more detail, although there is not a great deal of change. The sabretache has now been abolished for mounted officers of Native Infantry regiments, although still retained in the British service for a year or two.

The 3rd and 9th Gurkha Rifles have their belts specified as 'black enamelled seal leather', while the remainder have black patent leather. The mountings and badges of the 2nd are given as bronze, while all others have silver.

For Native officers the special British officers' pattern tunic is no longer given for the 2nd, and all have a simple green tunic with regimental facing with black lace on collar and cuffs. The cuffs are pointed for all except the 1st and 2nd who have the former slashed cuff piped in scarlet.

The 1899 Regulations laid down exact patterns for the design, and wear, of the various badges and devices of the Gurkha regiments, on buttons, helmets, waist-plates, forage caps, field caps, pouches, and belts. Lack of space precludes quotation here, but the following is an extract from the section, 'Uniform of British Officers serving with Regiments dressed in Green' in the volume dealing with the Punjab Frontier Force, and thus referring to the 5th Goorkha Regiment at that date:

'Officers belonging to regiments dressed in green wear green uniforms of the pattern prescribed for regiments dressed in drab with regimental facings. Shoulder straps of Hussar pattern in black, with badges of rank in bronze; lace, black.'

Note: Punjab Frontier Force regiments dressed in drab had the hussar-type tunic with loops of square cord as described for Bengal regiments in green. The facings and lace of the 5th Goorkha Regiment were black and ornaments silver. The following variations were sanctioned:

Trousers and Pantaloons – In the 5th Goorkha regiment the lace down the side seams is 2 inches wide.

Dress Spurs – In the 5th Goorkhas are flat, straight and silver-plated.

Patrol Jacket – In the 5th Goorkha regiment has plain pockets, and a fern leaf pattern in mohair braid down the back from the bottom of collar.

Active Service Cap – Green cloth, with silver bugle on black cord boss.

Helmet – In the 5th Goorkhas covered with rifle-green cloth, with silver spike, dome and chin-strap.

* * *

There are in the 1913 Regulations some interesting additional details of the dress of Native officers. Hot weather and service dress is given as khaki, regimental pattern. The tunic is thus described:

Gurkha and Garhwal Rifle Regiments with black facings –
Cloth green superfine, with a piping of facing cloth ¼ inch wide down the left front, skirts, pleats, and centre of back, and from bottom button to the bottom of tunic on the right front. Collar 1½ inches in depth made of facing cloth, slightly rounded at front, and fastened with one hook and eye with half inch black silk lace all round. The cuffs are rounded off at hind arm seam and the lace carried down each side of the seam, finishing off inside cuff. Eight large horn buttons, Rifle pattern, down front, two at skirt behind, and two small horn buttons Rifle pattern, for shoulder-straps. The sleeves and fronts are lined with white cotton; waist-hook in seam both sides. A pocket up and down inside left breast.

Gurkha Rifle Regiments, with scarlet facings:
1st Gurkha Rifles – Instead of tunic the patrol jacket as for the King's Royal Rifle Corps.
2nd Gurkha Rifles – As for British officers.
Trousers – Gurkha and Garhwal Rifles: Serge, green, dark. *Indian officers* – Fly-fronted, one small fob pocket on right side, side seam plain.
2nd Gurkha Rifles – As for British officers.

The helmet worn by British officers was no longer the same shape as the home service spiked helmet of the British infantry officer, but was now 'Wolseley' pattern, having a wider and more horizontal brim. Lines were now specified of black cord – 'Gurkha regiments and 55th Rifles, as for British Rifle regiments. Hooked on the right breast 2 inches from the seam of the sleeve.' For the 2nd all was to be as for the King's Royal Rifle Corps.

During the First World War uniform was worn according to the theatre; thus shorts and long puttees and shirt-sleeves or drill jackets were worn in the tropics, while warmer woollen clothing had to be issued for wear in France. The slouch hat turned up on the left side was widely worn, with sometimes a distinctive flash and/or badge on the upturned brim. Thus a rifleman of the 1st is shown in a painting with a red flash upon which is a crossed-kukries badge; the 1/8th appear to have worn a red hackle above a scarlet patch, while the 2nd battalion had a red pompon. Some regiments did not turn up the brim.

The equipment worn is of some interest; certain regiments, e.g. the 7th, wearing cavalry leather bandoliers, and two additional cavalry-pattern pouches as worn on the bandolier, one on each side of the waist-belt.

The slouch hat had been introduced some time prior to the First World War (Carman states in 1907) and one of the superb paintings by Lovett in MacMunn's *Armies of India* shows Gurkhas of the 4th in action on the frontier wearing the slouch hat, bandolier equipment, khaki shorts, jacket of drill, and long khaki puttees. A British officer wears the same except for a khaki Wolseley helmet. He also appears to be wearing an ammunition bandolier. This was the dress worn to France in 1914, and in the Middle East.

*   *   *

Between the two world wars khaki was the general wear for all occasions both hot weather and cold, with few exceptions. The introduction of the grey flannel shirt for drill and service wear introduced a new colour and a most comfortable garment, the colour varying slightly but on the

King's Indian Orderly Officers, 1905. From left: Major A. P. Bateman-Champion, 1/3rd; Subadar Jab Lal Rai, 2/10th; Subadar Nawal Singh Rawa, I.O.M., 8th; Subadar Kirpa Ram Thapa, O.B.I., I.O.M., 1/2nd; and Subadar-Major Karin Sing Gurung, 1/1st. (Courtesy, Colonel Frank Wilson)

33

whole a silver or blue-grey. This was worn summer and winter. Review order was well-starched drill shorts. Some regimental bands returned to full dress; e.g. the 7th or the 8th, I do not recall which for certain, in Razmak in the 1930s, whose band had rifle-green Highland doublets with white piping round the edge and edging the double 'castellated' wings. The Pipe-Major wore a silver gorget, the last to be worn in the British Empire. The reason had long been forgotten. Officers were allowed to wear full dress at levees, or on suitable occasions if serving as A.D.C. or King's Orderly Officer, and of course, officers had the pre-war mess kit.

Bodyguards, bands, and personal staff to the Viceroy and governors were to continue wearing full dress, and the Resident to Nepal's bodyguard.

It should be remembered that in peacetime British officers or Gurkha officers may appear in costumes which seem most unusual, and which can usually be accounted for if the complex and detailed regulations pertaining to staff officers are consulted, since A.D.C.s to various dignitaries and officers of the General Staff were authorized numerous orders of dress not worn with their regiments such as dress helmets and accoutrements, frock-coats, white drill summer patrols, etc.

The 1932 Regulations are the last to give detailed descriptions of the various regimental badges before the Second World War and subsequent partition, so it is worth noting these in detail:

1ST K.G.O. GURKHA RIFLES (THE MALAUN REGIMENT)

Buttons – In black horn, crossed khukris, edge downwards with '1' in the upper angle and a stringed bugle in the lower angle.

On collar of tunic and mess-jacket – Nil.

On collar of service dress – Nil.

On head-dress (helmet, or felt hat) – On helmet – in oxidized silver, crossed khukris with the plume of the Prince of Wales in the upper angle; in the lower angle a stringed bugle surmounted by the figure '1'. (*Note:* An amendment of April 1938 specified 'on the white full dress helmet'.)

On cap – In silver, on a red boss, crossed khukris with the plume of the Prince of Wales in the upper angle; on the lower angle a stringed bugle surmounted by the figure '1'.

On Kilmarnock cap – In silver, crossed khukris, edge downwards with the plume of the Prince of Wales in the upper angle. The figure '1' below the centre of the coronet. (*Note:* An amendment of April 1938 altered this to be the same as that worn 'on the cap' above.)

1st Battalion, 8th Gurkha Rifles, 1914. This group shows various ranks in assorted costumes. On the left the drummer and piper and the Native officer wear full dress of rifle-green faced black, with black puttees and belts and silver or white metal buttons. The Highland jackets are piped white, the pipe-tassels and cords are dark green. The Gurkha officer in the centre wears light khaki drill service dress with black buttons and boots and Sam Browne belt, the latter with both braces, and a khaki haversack. The revolver on the right is almost invisible but the ammunition-pouch on the left is clear. The drill havildar wears guard order. The naik (corporal) wears light khaki drill service dress, cut in pullover style, with buttons to the mid-chest and side vents at the bottom. His brown leather equipment is of cavalry pattern, with brass buckles. The last figure is in regimental mufti – plain clothes – with an undress Kilmarnock, black stockings, and regimental boots. (National Army Museum)

1. **Centre of officer's pouch-belt badge, 1st King George's Own Gurkha Rifles, 1913**
2. **Badge on buttons from 1913 – 2nd King Edward's Own Gurkha Rifles**
3. **Helmet badge, 3rd Queen Alexandra's Own Gurkha Rifles, 1911. Today the Lions of Asoka and a star replace the crown and As, since the regiment is in Indian service**
4. **Helmet and cap badge, 4th Prince of Wales's Own Gurkha Rifles – silver from 1839. No plumes now worn**
5. **Buttons, helmet, and waist-plate (Gurkha officers only) and forage cap – 5th Royal Gurkha Rifles (Frontier Force). The Lions of Asoka have now been added**
6. **6th Queen Elizabeth's Own Gurkha Rifles, badge worn since 1956**
7. **7th Duke of Edinburgh's Own Gurkha Rifles, badge worn since 1959**
8. **Officer's pouch-belt badge, 8th Gurkha Rifles, 1911**
9. **Buttons, forage cap and field cap, 9th Gurkha Rifles, 1911. Crown now replaced by Lions of Asoka**
10. **10th Princess Mary's Own Gurkha Rifles, 1949**
11. **Staff Band, current cap badge**
12. **Gurkha Engineers, cap badge**
13. **Gurkha Military Police, cap badge**
14. **Gurkha Army Transport Corps cap badge**
15. **Gurkha Signals cap badge**

2ND KING EDWARD'S OWN GURKHA RIFLES (THE SIRMOOR RIFLES)

On buttons – In black horn crossed khukris edge downwards surmounted by the Royal and Imperial cipher of King Edward VII.

On collar of white summer mess-jacket (only) – In silver the plume of His Royal Highness the Prince of Wales.

On collar of service dress – Nil.

On head-dress – on white full-dress helmet – In silver the plume of H.R.H. the Prince of Wales.

On cap – The plume of His Royal Highness the Prince of Wales, in silver on a red boss.

On Kilmarnock cap for Gurkha ranks – The plume of His Royal Highness the Prince of Wales in bronze.

3RD QUEEN ALEXANDRA'S OWN GURKHA RIFLES

On the buttons – In black horn, crossed khukris, edge upwards with '3' in the upper angle.

On collar of mess-jacket only – The cipher of Queen Alexandra ensigned with the Imperial Crown.

On collar of service jacket – Nil.

On felt hat – In black metal, the cipher of Queen Alexandra ensigned with the Imperial Crown.

On cap – In silver, the cipher of Queen Alexandra ensigned with the Imperial Crown. (On buttons in front, two crossed khukris enclosing a '3' in silver.)*

4TH PRINCE OF WALES'S OWN GURKHAS

On buttons – In black horn, crossed khukris surmounted by the plume of His Royal Highness the Prince of Wales. In the lower angle of the khukris, the figure 'IV'.

On collar of tunic and mess-jacket – In silver the plume of His Royal Highness the Prince of Wales.

On collar of service dress – Nil.

On head-dress (amendment of April 1939 adds 'on white full dress helmet') – In bronze, crossed khukris, surmounted by the plume of His Royal Highness the Prince of Wales. In the lower angle of the khukris, the figure '4'. (*Note:* The same amendment alters 'silver' to 'bronze'.)

On cap – In silver, as on collar of tunic and mess-jacket. (*Note:* The boss was black.)

5TH ROYAL GURKHA RIFLES (FRONTIER FORCE)

On buttons – In black horn, crossed khukris with '5' in the upper angle, surmounted by the Royal Crest.

* *On Kilmarnock cap* – In white metal, crossed khukris, edge upwards with '3' in upper angle surmounted by the cipher of Queen Alexandra ensigned with the Imperial Crown.

On collar of tunic and mess-jacket – In silver, crossed khukris with '5' in the upper angle, surmounted by the Royal Crest.

On the collar of service jacket – Nil.

On head-dress – As in column 3 (e.g. collar) to be worn on white full-dress helmet.

On cap – As in column 3 (e.g. collar). (*Note:* The boss was black.)

6TH GURKHA RIFLES

On buttons – In black horn, crossed khukris, edge downwards and '6' between the handles.

On collar of tunic and mess-jacket – In silver, crossed khukris, edge downwards and '6' between the handles.

On collar of service jacket – Nil.

On helmet – Nil.

On cap – In silver, crossed khukris, edge downwards and '6' between the handles below a scroll inscribed 'GURKHA RIFLES'. (*Note:* Amendment No. 25 of November 1932 deleted the reference to a scroll inscribed Gurkha Rifles, while a later amendment, No. 33 of April 1938 added, after the word 'handles', 'on a black boss'.)

7TH GURKHA RIFLES

On buttons – In black horn crossed khukris, edge upwards with '7' in upper angle.

On collars – Nil.

On helmet – In silver, crossed khukris, edge upwards with '7' in the upper angle.

This fine Caton Woodville sketch shows Gurkhas in action during the First World War. It has an unusual central figure – the havildar-major is not often the centrepiece of a picture. Note that he has two miniature kukris attached to his fighting weapon, while the bugler behind him has only one and other ranks have none: the significance of this feature is not clear. (National Army Museum)

British officer in review order, 1920s; a sketch by Colonel Borrowman of the 1/4th Gurkhas. The khaki helmet has a narrow leather binding at the edge. A khaki shirt and tie is worn under a baratfea jacket. The Sam Browne belt is black with white metal mounts, and boots, gaiters, and spur-straps are all black. The sword-knot is black, and the revolver lanyard probably the same, although the 5th had red. The scabbard is black leather with steel mounts and the spurs steel. Shoulder-titles and rank-badges are black. (National Army Museum)

On cap – In silver, as on helmet. (*Note:* The field cap had a black boss for the badge.)

Note: An amendment No. 34 of April 1938 altered the entry about the head-dress to read: '*On felt hat, 1st Battalion* – In black metal crossed khukries, edge uppermost with "7" in the upper angle. *2nd Battalion* – In silver, crossed khukries, edge uppermost with "7" in the upper angle.'

To the column 6 (the cap) was added: '*On Kilmarnock cap* – In silver, crossed khukries edge uppermost with "7" in the upper angle.'

8TH GURKHA RIFLES

On buttons – In black horn, crossed khukris with '8' in upper angle.

On collar of tunic and mess-jacket – In silver crossed khukris with '8' in the upper angle. (*Note:* Altered by amendment No. 35 of 1938 to 'Nil'.)

On collar of service dress – Nil.

On head-dress – Nil.

On cap – In silver on a black bar as on collar of mess-jacket. (*Note:* Amendment No. 35 of 1938 adds '*On Kilmarnock cap* – In silver, crossed khukries with "8" in upper angle.'

On officers' forage cap – As above (in miniature) mounted on a red silk cord boss.

9TH GURKHA RIFLES

On buttons – In black horn, crossed khukris, edge downwards with '9' in lower angle.

On collar of tunic and mess-jacket – In silver, crossed khukris, with a crown in the upper angle, and '9' in lower angle.

On collar of service dress – Nil.

On helmet – In silver, crossed khukris edge downwards with '9' in lower angle.

On cap – In silver on a black bar as on helmet.

Note: The original entries for this regiment were so full of misprints as to be almost meaningless. An order, No. 50 of October 1938, finally made sense of them. Collar badges were worn on mess-jackets only, the head-dress badge was to be worn on helmet and Kilmarnock, in white metal, and the silver cap badge was to be worn on a 'black boss' not 'bar'.

10TH GURKHA RIFLES

On buttons – In black horn, a bugle suspended by knotted strings crossed by a khukri, edge downwards.

On collar openners, jacket only – In silver, a bugle suspended by knotted strings crossed by a khukri edge downwards. (What *collar openners* are eludes me.)

On collar of service dress – Nil.

On helmet – Crossed khukris, edge downwards and '15' in upper angle. (The printer had evidently run amuck, and an order No. 20 of September 1937 stated the helmet badge was to be the same as on collars.

On forage cap – *Gurkha officers, Kilmarnock cap* – In silver as on collar, on a black boss.

(*Note:* The boss was worn only on the forage cap, not on the Kilmarnock.)

*　　*　　*

In wartime it is every man for himself, and regulations tend to be forgotten if not deliberately flouted while each man looks to his own comfort and each C.O. to the practical clothing of his unit. But even in war some line must be drawn, and in a Special Indian Army Order No. 7/S of October

1942 Lord Wavell endeavoured to draw it. The object was to 'reduce the number of variations in patterns of uniforms' and to 'eliminate' such monstrosities as suede shoes and boots, short-sleeved shirts (mosquitoes liked these), corduroy trousers (which wore remarkably well) and 'irregular garters, flashes, etc.'

As usual the wearing of unauthorized items was forbidden, and as usual they flourished. But there is a particularly interesting para (5):

'b. When travelling by air. Except when expressly authorized by G.H.Q. uniform will NOT be worn by serving personnel of H.M. Forces travelling on any journey by air which entails passage through a neutral country (Egypt and Iraq excepted).'

Further puzzle: Shorts were not to be worn in Lisbon, but the provisions of this order did not apply to W.A.C.(I)!

Briefly the dress laid down was as follows: In hot climate for all ranks: cellular bush-shirts, trousers or shorts (the former after sunset, because of mosquitoes), anklets or short puttees with hose-tops. In cold climate: battledress with boots and

A Gurkha havildar, 1945 – instantly recognizable as the work of Colonel Borrowman, and typifying the archetypal Gurkha remembered by all who served alongside them in the Second World War. The khaki battledress was often manufactured in Australia. The camouflage net fitted over the bush hat is interesting. (National Army Museum)

Gurkha orderly, 1945, in the dress which might be worn by the colonel's stick orderly of the day, possibly at the depot: another fine sketch by Colonel Borrowman of the 1/4th. The rifleman wears light khaki drill bush-shirt and slacks, with the usual khaki webbing belt and gaiters; the buckle, dull by regulation, was often polished bright. The regimental badge in silver is worn on a black cloth patch on the khaki serge beret; the black cane is silver-mounted. (National Army Museum)

King's Indian orderly officers, 1938. From left: Subadar-Major and Honorary Lieutenant Shamsheh Sing Boima, O.B.I., 2nd; Subadar Bal Bahadur Khattri, I.D.S.M., 2/9th; Major C. M. H. Wingfield, 1/2nd; Subadar Bhawar Sing Rai, O.B.I., I.O.M., 1/10th; and Subadar Major Dalbur Chand, O.B.I., I.D.S.M., 1/5th. The outstanding feature of this picture is Major Wingfield's head-dress, an astrakhan cap of the same pattern as worn by the 60th. The plume was red over black, and the small silver regimental badge on the boss is as worn on the forage cap. Note how clear the dicing now appears on the left-hand cap. (Courtesy, Colonel Frank Wilson)

anklets or short puttees (on parade); or heavy flannel shirts, pullover jerseys, shorts or trousers and anklets, or short puttees with hosetops. When full equipment was not worn on duty, the belt alone must be worn, and trousers must not have turnups, under pain of death! There was much latitude for officers and other ranks on static staff or garrison duties, such as the wearing of stockings and shoes with shorts when not on parade.

Divisional signs were to be worn by all ranks, also on the greatcoat, and new badges of rank for Indian officers were introduced:

Risaldar and Subadar-Majors – Khaki detachable shoulder-strap with three braid bands, each band

consisting of three strands of braid, red, yellow, red, with a miniature silver crown on each band. *Risaldar and Subadar* – Two braids with a miniature silver star on each.
Jemadar – One braid band as above with a miniature silver star.

After the Second World War full-dress uniforms as hitherto understood virtually vanished, and an outfit known as No. 1 dress (based, one is tempted to believe, upon the London Transport model) became almost universal throughout the British Army of which those Gurkhas remaining outside the Partition of India now formed a part.

Service dress followed the current fashions and exigencies of the service, proving practical and serviceable, which is all that should be asked of service dress.

PIPE BANNERS

Mr W. Y. Carman of the National Army Museum gives some details, writing in the *Bulletin of the Military Historical Society* in November 1962. He gives no date but states that the 6th had a dark green banner with the crowned kukris over a '6' in red, while the 7th had a similar banner with the regimental badge and battle-honour scrolls, and the 10th their bugle-horn badge also between battle honours. All these were guidon or split-tail pattern.

The new banners presented to the 6th at about the date of Mr Carman's article were exceptionally fine and were far more like regimental colours than is usual. One was green, the other blue. Both are guidon-shaped, that is to say have a double-pointed bottom, and each has a crown and rose, and a thistle-and-shamrock wreath embroidered in coloured silk after the time-honoured design of British infantry colours. Both are fringed. In the centre of one, all upon scarlet, is 'E II R' within a garter bearing the title, VI QUEEN ELIZABETH'S OWN GURKHA RIFLES. The second or blue banner has the centre regimental motif of crossed kukris, edge downwards, ensigned with a crown, and '6' in the lower angle, and the battalion number 'I' in the top corner.

The 7th, who became the Duke of Edinburgh's Own in 1959, were given a banner with the Duke's coat of arms emblazoned thereon, the obverse being green with the regimental badge between two columns of battle honours, and green and white fringe.

The 10th had recently a guidon-pattern banner with the full regimental badge and fringed with a mixed fringe of metal and a colour in true cavalry guidon style.

The Engineers' banner is described as on a dark ground a gilt grenade over silver kukris and a dark red (?) fringe.

Finally, the 2/6th have a banner with the regimental crest on one side, but upon the other appears the Prussian eagle and title upon a scroll of the 14/20th Hussars, commemorating the Battle of Medecina in Italy, when in 1945 the 14/20th's armoured carriers took the 2/6th into action. From a photograph the badge upon the pipe-major's black sword-belt is exactly of the pattern described for officers' pouch-belts in the 1914 Regulations.

Drum-major of the Gurkha Signals, in white full-dress patrol jacket worn with white shorts and black boots and puttees. The black sash is embroidered in gold and silver, the crown in silk of 'proper' colours. The silver-topped staff does not have twisted chains. The gold-on-black chevrons can be seen on the right forearm. (Army Public Relations)

THE TARTANS USED BY GURKHA PIPE BANDS*

The 8th Gurkhas use a 'Universal' tartan that appears to be a variation on the Black Watch or the Sutherland tartan, on bagpipes (covers) and as ribbons. The 9th use none. The 1st Battalion of the 1st use 'Childers' – a transposed Mackintosh tartan. The 2nd Battalion use MacKenzie, both battalions using the tartan as plaids, pipe-bag covers and ribbons. Neither the 1st nor 2nd Battalions of the 4th use tartan. The 2nd Battalion of the 5th use Black Watch for plaid, bag, and ribbons, and the 6th Gurkha Rifles use Black Watch for bags and ribbons only.

THE KUKRI

The kukri knife, the national weapon of the Gurkhas, has attracted myths in proportion to its fame. Two may be mentioned: that the kukri may be thrown, and returns to its owner's hand like a boomerang after filleting an enemy; and that for 'religious reasons' the kukri may be drawn only to spill blood, and that the owner must therefore nick his finger each time he draws it to clean the blade. The truth is less colourful, for which the Gurkhas must be thankful – one can pass a heavy, razor-sharp blade across one's finger only a limited number of times without running a severe risk of digital amputation.

* From *Clans, Septs and Regiments of the Scottish Highlands*, Frank Adams, 1934.

The kukri is produced in many sizes for many types of task, but the unique 'dog-leg' shape is constant. The blade swells from a narrow neck into a very broad, down-swept leaf shape, which tapers again to a sharp point. The back edge is unsharpened and very thick and the lower or cutting edge is razor-sharp. The steel is of excellent temper, and the great weight imparted by the thick back edge makes the kukri a terrifyingly effective chopping-knife. Its balance is such that throwing is quite impossible. It is used for all the dozen and one tasks which crop up in camp and in the field – clearing undergrowth, chopping firewood, and so forth. It is also the Gurkha soldier's preferred hand-to-hand weapon in combat. From the earliest days of the Gurkha battalions in British service up to the present day, the kukri has been carried in a sheath on the waist-belt alongside the soldier's regulation weapons and equipment. At close quarters, especially in jungle or other thickly wooded country, a skilled man can wield the kukri with greater ease and more devastating effect than a rifle and fixed bayonet. For all his small stature the Gurkha has immense wiry strength, and there are numerous reliable accounts of enemy heads struck off at a single blow. The enemies against whom the Gurkha has been sent, especially in recent generations, have tended to find this more than a little unnerving.

Pipe-major of the Gurkha Signals. The magnificent pipe-banner bears the arms of the Princess Royal, at that time the Colonel-in-Chief of the Royal Corps of Signals to which the Gurkha unit is affiliated. The tartan is Grant, and the 'tourie' on the Kilmarnock light blue. The corps has a second banner, dark red with a gilt crown over a silver Mercury above crossed kukris edge upwards. (Army Public Relations)